T0224932

Agile Software Development with HP Agile Manager

Liran Tal

Apress®

Agile Software Development with HP Agile Manager

ISBN-13 (pbk): 978-1-4842-1035-2

ISBN-13 (electronic): 978-1-4842-1034-5

Managing Director: Welmoed Spahr
Lead Editor: James DeWolf
Development Editor: Douglas Pundick
Technical Reviewer: Sergiu Ciupe
Editorial Board: Steve Anglin, Mark Beckner, Gary Cornell, Louise Corrigan, Jim DeWolf, Jonathan Gennick, Robert Hutchinson, Susan McDermott, Michelle Lowman, James Markham, Matthew Moodie, Jeffrey Pepper, Douglas Pundick, Ben Renow-Clarke, Gwenan Spearing, Matt Wade, Steve Weiss
Coordinating Editor: Melissa Maldonado
Copy Editor: Kim Wimpsett
Compositor: SPi Global
Indexer: SPi Global
Artist: SPi Global

Distributed to the book trade worldwide by Springer Science+Business Media New York, 233 Spring Street, 6th Floor, New York, NY 10013. Phone 1-800-SPRINGER, fax (201) 348-4505, e-mail orders-ny@springer-sbm.com, or visit www.springeronline.com. Apress Media, LLC is a California LLC and the sole member (owner) is Springer Science + Business Media Finance Inc (SSBM Finance Inc). SSBM Finance Inc is a Delaware corporation.

For information on translations, please e-mail rights@apress.com, or visit www.apress.com.

Apress and friends of ED books may be purchased in bulk for academic, corporate, or promotional use. eBook versions and licenses are also available for most titles. For more information, reference our Special Bulk Sales–eBook Licensing web page at www.apress.com/bulk-sales.

Any source code or other supplementary material referenced by the author in this text is available to readers at www.apress.com. For detailed information about how to locate your book's source code, go to www.apress.com/source-code/.

Contents at a Glance

Contents

About the Author

Liran Tal is leading the R&D engineering team for HP Software's enterprise content market place, distribution, and collaboration platform, where he strives for improved agile software development by adopting scrum processes, creating multinational feature teams, and managing the group's agile workflow through HP's Agile Manager software tool. He loves mentoring and empowering team members, driving for better code methodology, and seeking out innovative solutions to support business strategies.

In his group, Liran plays a key role in system architecture design, shaping the technology strategy from planning and development to deployment and maintenance in HP's IaaS cloud, spanning a combined technology stack of Drupal/PHP, Java, and NodeJS.

Being an avid supporter and contributor to the open source movement, in 2007 he redefined network RADIUS management by founding and developing daloRADIUS, a world-recognized and industry-leading open source project (www.daloradius.com).

In his spare time, Liran is a top contributor to the open source MEAN.io and MEAN.js full-stack JavaScript frameworks. Expert in Drupal, he previously authored the book *Drupal 7 Media* and technically reviewed more than half a dozen other books about Drupal, MongoDB, and NodeJS.

Liran graduated *cum laude* with a bachelor's degree in business and information systems analysis and enjoys spending his time with his beloved wife, Tal, and his magical son, Ori. Among other things, his hobbies include playing the guitar, hacking all things Linux, and continuously experimenting and contributing to open source and web development projects.

You can connect with Liran at www.linkedin.com/in/talliran or e-mail him at liran@enginx.com.

About the Technical Reviewer

Sergiu Ciupe has been doing software quality assurance for eight years. He currently works at HP Software, leading the QA team of HP Live Network, which is a project involving a combined technology stack (featuring Drupal, Java, JavaScript, Node, js, Python, and MongoDB) and geographically distributed teams, and he uses Agile Manager to streamline this elaborated R&D process. Sergiu is involved in all development phases, being able to see the benefits of using Agile Manager daily. He has a master's degree in software engineering and a bachelor's degree in computer science and loves skiing and traveling to discover different cultures.

Acknowledgments

I would like to thank my manager, Yaniv Bigger, for being more than just that—for being a great coach and mentor, for enabling an environment of opportunities where I can grow and extend my skills, and for inspiring me with the way he leads our R&D group at HP. Thanks for being a great teacher and motivator. I always find new things I can learn from you.

To my team, thank you for being diverse, unique, exceptional, and a company of technological heroes, each in your own way. Your support and trust have contributed to improving myself as a leader and mentor.

Lastly, I would like to express my gratitude to James DeWolf and Melissa Maldonado from Apress who were onboard with this book from the start, who supported me throughout the publishing path, and who were dedicated to seeing it through. Moreover, this book's top quality has been assured thanks to Sergiu Ciupe, who suggested great ideas duringthe review process and provided meaningful insights.

Introduction

Agile development practices have been widely adopted in a variety of organizations, yet only a few tools are available to help make the practical process of managing agile teams less painful and more successful. HP Agile Manager is a purpose-built SaaS-based agile planning tool that provides a simpler, smarter way to manage collaborative development. Agile Manager can work for small startups and midsize teams and can scale up for bigger organizations as a cost-effective and flexible tool to apply agile techniques to improve your software development process.

This book combines agile software development practices with HP's Agile Manager tool, when used as a SaaS product or an on-premise solution, and will explain how to master key functionalities of Agile Manager. It teaches you how to build and plan releases, create a product's backlog, and manage day-to-day R&D activity such as addressing user stories and defects and reviewing the team activity with the help of informative dashboards. While this book is not designed to teach agile software development *per se*, it starts out with a chapter that covers agile software development practices and specifically focuses on the Scrum agile methodology and its related concepts.

Who This Book Is For

This book assumes no previous knowledge of agile tools, or agile in general, so developers, quality engineers, development team leaders, and other stakeholders in an R&D team will find this book serves them well in learning and applying agile methodologies in their teams and in successfully building and adopting an agile development framework in their software projects. This book will also be of great help for teams already using an agile framework who want to further improve on their delivery with a more flexible agile tool such as Agile Manager.

Young team leaders and engineering managers will especially benefit from this book by learning and understanding how to adopt Scrum agile processes for successfully delivering results in their teams.

How This Book Is Structured

This book is designed to walk you through the software development stages ofanagile software methodology. It begins by laying the foundation for the agile philosophy and continues with signingup for and setting up HP's Agile Manager tool to manage a software project. It continues with chapters covering how to create the product's backlog, how to create themes and features, how to manage sprints, and how to streamline the R&D team's activities with user stories and defects. Finally, the book covers how to use dashboards and widgets to track and monitor real-time team activity and ends by reviewing online resources for further learning about Agile Manager's features, support, and the community around it.

CHAPTER 1

The Agile World

To begin your journey with managing agile teams and using Agile Manager for streamlining an agile workflow, you'll dive into the agile world by learning about the concepts, terminology, and the agile software development methodology.

In this chapter, you'll learn the basics of the agile philosophy and working principles to set the mood for the rest of your agile journey. We'll cover the following topics:

- Introducing the basic concepts and traits of the agile philosophy

- Reviewing agile terminology, including roles in software development

- Reviewing agile software models

Introducing Agile Software Development

The prominent software development methodology in the 20th century was the Waterfall process model, which employs a sequential design and development process that originated in the manufacturing and construction industry. While the Waterfall process is still used throughout the industry today in some software projects, the agile philosophy, introduced in 2001, challenges the norm of developing software projects by providing a less rigid, more flexible framework for developing software, where a shippable and deliverable product is achieved quicker through progressing research and development (R&D) iterations.

Origins of Waterfall Model

The basics of Waterfall model workflows are about setting up a pipeline process chain, which begins with a requirements phase and early planning step that may account for up to 30 percent of the time invested in the project. The rationale behind investing so much time in ironing out the requirements lies in the claim, per Rapid Development: Taming Wild Software Schedules (Microsoft Press, 1996), that a bug found in the early stages of requirements analysis is cheaper in terms of cost and R&D effort than the same bug discovered later in the process.

Note The Waterfall model is one of many software project models available for anyone to adopt, and modifications on the original Waterfall model include the Spiral model, the more current V-model, and the Modified Waterfall.

Software projects then continue with the rest of the phases of software modeling, building, and testing, and finally continue with the last phase of delivering the final product and maintenance, as shown in Figure 1-1.

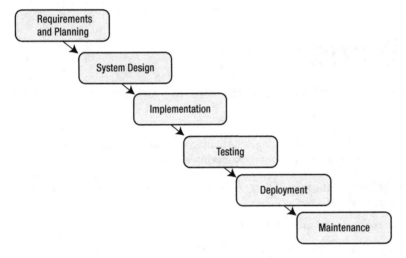

Figure 1-1. *Agile software development: Waterfall model*

Software projects developed with the Waterfall model provide a simpler approach to software development life cycles and provide solid requirements and general documentation assets throughout their initial phases, which enables new team members to easily join a project.

However, the following are the disadvantages of the Waterfall model:

- *Inflexible*: The Waterfall is unresponsive to changes. Once the specification requirements phase has locked in all the planned features, the project continues until completion.

- *Prone to bottlenecks and delays*: If an issue is detected at a late phase, such as in development or testing, this affects the entire process line because the phases are quite sequential, and it may introduce a significant delay time.

- *Late product delivery*: Only the completion of the final phases of the software project provide a working, deliverable product.

■ **Note** Today, you may still witness the Waterfall software development model employed for large projects or for corporations that haven't chosen to adopt a more agile workflow. Other reasons for organizations to employ a Waterfall process model is when technology, requirements, and product specification and definition are all stable, known, and considered constant. In other occasions, the Waterfall method may simply be a requirement of some governments and industries.

The Agile World of Software Development

Entering into the 21st century, in 2001 the first concepts of agile software development were introduced in the form of the Agile Manifesto (http://agilemanifesto.org). Some of the key values to the philosophy behind agile development processes are as follows:

- **Individuals and interactions** over processes and tools

- **Working software** over comprehensive documentation

- **Customer collaboration** over contract negotiation

- **Responding to change** over following a plan

These values mitigate and address concerns in previous, more rigid software development methodologies such as the original Waterfall model. It does not mean that processes, tools, documentation, or following a plan has no value but simply that the agile philosophy values these less when compared with other key values.

R&D **individuals and interactions**, collaboration, and continuous frontal team updates help to flush out any obstacles team members have and give room for ideas exchange and immediate feedback from teammates. It should be noted that agile methodologies don't reject tools or processes altogether but rather hint that fostering team members' interaction, as shown in Figure 1-2, is of higher value, and interactions shouldn't be replaced entirely by any tool or process.

Figure 1-2. *Individuals and interactions over processes and tools*

Having **working software**, even if it provides minimal value to the customer, is preferred over developing and documenting an entire software project whose life span can be relatively long and may turn out to be partially irrelevant when delivery is made. In other words, documenting every single part of the system by writing a top-notch requirements specification for every aspect in the product that will cover every feature to be developed is time-consuming and may often turn out to be a throwaway task because user requirements change; in addition, it's crucial to get users to interact with your software as soon as possible to be able to collect feedback and valuable input.

Documentation should not be disregarded or overlooked, though. It should exist, but it shouldn't be comprehensive in a way that stalls development or stalls the shipping of a minimal product to the customer to gain feedback. As shown in Figure 1-3, a product can be minimally functional and deliver customer value.

Figure 1-3. *Working software over comprehensive documentation*

Where contract negotiation limits the evolution of a software project because it ties down the agreed-upon features and developed content, agile promotes **collaboration with customers** to understand ongoing needs, reprioritization of features, and product vision for market alignment. Traditional software development models would lock in the customer to a feature set, and only then the project could continue with further design, development, and delivery. This meant that customers could evaluate the product only after everything had been developed and delivered and at a very late phase find out that the developers made bad decisions or that they were totally off with the market alignment and feature set. As shown in Figure 1-4, a customer's voice should be highly regarded and carefully examined, which can impact a product's feature set and vision altogether.

Figure 1-4. *Customer collaboration over contract negotiation*

All of these values are about being able to **respond to change** as software develops. Change should be embraced and prepared for with risk planning and modular, flexible software design. It is key to understand and accept that software evolves as users interact with it, and planned features may get thrown away or reprioritized. Agile software development acknowledges this ever-changing climate in software projects and offers solutions through processes to streamline these changes successfully.

Agile Flavors

The agile software development philosophy sets the mood for implementing the processes through the key values and principles. To support these values and build on the original agile principles, an emergence of agile methodologies and frameworks came to life to offer guidelines and lightweight processes to achieve agile development. These methodologies are also referred to as *flavors* of agile software development.

While there are many agile flavors, such as the more popular Scrum, Kanban, Extreme Programming (XP), and Feature-Driven Development (FDD), we won't cover all of them. Rather, we'll focus on Scrum, which is considered a common practice and which Agile Manager provides the toolbox for. Here are short reviews of selected agile methodologies:

- *Scrum*: In Scrum, products (or projects) are divided into iterative and time-boxed work units, referred to as *sprints*, which are typically two weeks long. A repetitive cycle composed of feature planning, user stories estimation, R&D work of developers and QA, and demos and retrospectives forms an iteration in which a potentially shippable product value can be met and delivered to the customer in minimal time.

- *Kanban*: Similar to Scrum, Kanban is an iterative process methodology that facilitates the delivery of product value through emphasis on optimizing the process flow. To make sure the process flow is adhered to, Kanban promotes the use of visualization of the flow's pipeline, often referred to as the *task board*, organized from left to right in flow of completion order, such as items that are in-progress development, done, in-testing items, done, and deployment. Items are put on the board and are moved in sequence from one column to another as they progress through the pipeline flow until completion.

- *Scrumban*: Merging both Scrum and Kanban, the Scrumban methodology desires to adopt the best elements from both and aims to integrate the task board workflow with Scrum concepts and foster the visualization of items. To that end, Scrumban promotes daily updates, review, and retrospective processes and combines them with Kanban work-in-progress (WIP) capacity limits and clear stages of execution.

■ **Note**   Agile Manager also provides tools and workflows to effectively practice Kanban in your team, and even a Scrumban variation is quite common and well supported in the tool.

Practicing Scrum Agile Development

Scrum is a lightweight agile framework that is focused on making small teams work efficiently together to deliver a working product by employing methodologies and processes to streamline the work of the Scrum team for a successful software project.

The Scrum approach to software projects is through an iterative and incremental process, where team members continually work together to create a working product and continuously introspect the process for self-improvements. Figure 1-5 shows an example of such a process.

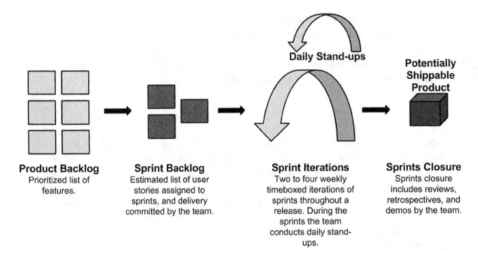

Figure 1-5. Example of agile Scrum development life cycle

■ **Note** While Scrum is well adopted and quite common in the technology industry, its processes can be customized and employed in other industries.

So you further understand the concepts of Scrum, we will lay the foundations of basic definitions in the world of an agile, and specifically Scrum, methodology.

Scrum Artifacts

The Scrum methodology identifies a few tangible deliverables that are the representations of specification requirements for the product or project.

The Product Backlog

The product backlog, as shown in Figure 1-6, is often referred to as the *general backlog* and is a prioritized list of requirements, or changes, that represent the desired feature set for the product. It is characterized as dynamic because requirements often change or are added.

Product Backlog Items

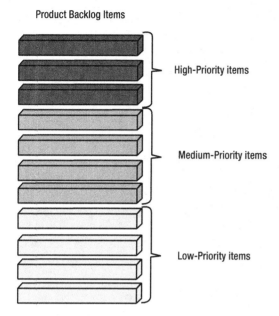

High-Priority items

Medium-Priority items

Low-Priority items

Figure 1-6. The product backlog

The content of the product backlog forms the basic idea pool for breaking the product backlog further into an organized set of deliverable value such as sprints and releases.

The following are backlog items that are referenced in the product backlog:

- *Themes*: Themes are general descriptive items for a focus area. For example, for a web application product, themes can be user management and messaging and notifications. Themes allow you to group similar interest area features.

- *Features*: Often referred to as *epics*, features describe a requirement in large and not so detailed specifics. Features can be thought of as a large set of tasks and items to develop (or large user stories) and are usually too large to complete in a single sprint. Features are broken down to smaller units called *user stories*, which are handled in the sprint backlog.

■ **Note** *Backlog grooming* is a common term for the practice of reorganizing the backlog items on the product backlog, such as reprioritizing them, removing them, creating new items, or correcting estimates. This activity is often referred to as the *backlog refinement meeting*.

The Sprint Backlog

Sprints are time-boxed, iterative periods in which the team works together to deliver a set of product value items.

Similar to the general backlog, the sprint backlog is a set of defined requirements that is much more detailed and descriptive that the team has identified, discussed, and planned for completion in a given sprint. These items should be developed, tested, documented, and then integrated to provide a shippable and deliverable product.

The following are backlog items that are referenced in the sprint backlog:

- *User stories*: User stories are customer-focused descriptions for functionality that needs to be achieved in order to answer a set of product requirements. Figure 1-7 shows an example of a user story.

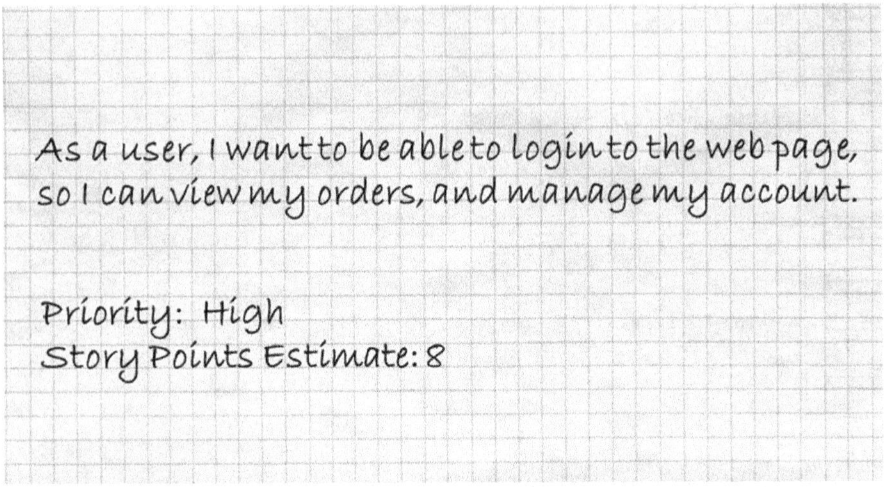

As a user, I want to be able to login to the web page, so I can view my orders, and manage my account.

Priority: High
Story Points Estimate: 8

Figure 1-7. *A typical user story*

- *Defects*: Defects and bugs are common backlog items that are tracked and logged by the QA team through sprint periods and are often used to indicate the quality of the product or developed functionality in a sprint.

■ **Note** Although it is common to use the term *bug* for describing problems in a feature or product, a bug and a defect aren't the same thing. A bug is the result of wrong or bad programming code, and a defect is a deviation from the requirements, a requirement that was not met, or a requirement that did not exist.

The following are general guidelines for user stories:

- *Simplicity*: User stories should be simple, short, concise, and often treated as small units of information that can fit on an A4 notecard.

- *Capture essential information*: User stories describe the who, what, and why of a requirement.

- *Estimated and prioritized*: User stories should be estimated using a measure like story points, which is a relative estimated effort, or using timed tasks. User stories should be small enough to complete within a single sprint; otherwise, they should be broken down into smaller user stories.

The Product Increment

A *product increment* is the set of product backlog items that have been completed in one or more sprints that provide value to the customer (see Figure 1-8). It is easy to understand product increments as releases, where each release, referred to as the *product increment* contributes to the final, more complete vision of the product and where real product value is provided in each release.

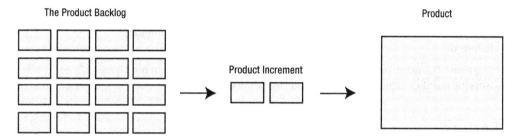

Figure 1-8. *The product increment*

Burndown Chart

The purpose of this chart is to represent the current state of the sprint in terms of the remaining work to be done. It is called a *burndown chart* because it should have a declining graph as the team walks toward the end of the sprint and work is decreasing toward completion (see Figure 1-9).

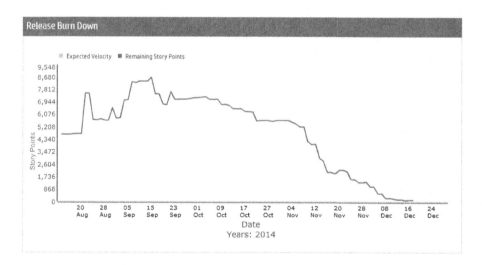

Figure 1-9. *The burndown chart*

Burndown charts show the remaining work on the y-axis and the sprint time length on the x-axis. On top of the actual remaining work items, the chart usually includes trend lines indicating the expected and actual remaining work and can be translated into the velocity of the team. That is, this is the speed in which backlog items are achieved throughout sprints.

Scrum Roles

The Scrum methodology defines a Scrum team that is composed of Scrum's own set of Scrum roles. These roles are not common titles like product manager or team leader.

- *Product owner*: The product owner manages the product backlog and ensures the backlog items are prioritized according to the product vision and are aligned with customer value and priority.

- *Scrum master*: The Scrum master is responsible for streamlining the Scrum team processes, activities, and practices to ensure that the Scrum methodology is followed.

- *The team*: The team includes the R&D team, developers, and QA team members working together to incrementally deliver shippable value products.

Scrum Sprints

In the Scrum methodology, software projects are facilitated through a predefined time window, usually several weeks long, of iterations that are referred to as *sprints*. Within these sprints, the team work together to achieve and complete parts of the project, through swift planning, R&D work, a closing retrospective, and demo sessions.

Figure 1-10 shows a simple and typical sprint iterative process; although the figure is incomplete, we'll fill in the details as we step you through the complete Scrum picture.

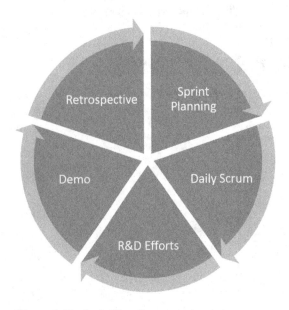

Figure 1-10. Sprint iterative concept

■ **Note**   Demo sessions at the end of each sprint are important and allow the product owner to assess the fulfilment of the sprint backlog.

Let's identify the sprint activities and characteristics that take place in the iterative process. Often these activities are also referred to as *ceremonies*.

Iterative Cycle

As Figure 1-10 shows, sprints are iterative cycles of activities, which commonly span two weeks to four weeks. Once you've identified the sprint time that is best for your team, the sprints form a fixed and repetitive time length for a release.

Sprint Planning

At the beginning of each sprint, you'll plan the content of the sprint, estimate efforts and time, and agree upon any content that can be achieved and delivered within the sprint.

A typical sprint planning session is held for one to two hours, where the team plans the user stories and commits on their delivery for the sprint.

■ **Note**   *Planning poker*, also referred to as *Scrum poker*, is a game that can be employed in sprint planning meetings, in which the Scrum team uses relative effort estimation measures referred to as *story points* to estimate the size of user stories. In the game, the team is faced with a user story, where each member puts face down a story point card, and when cards are revealed at once, the team begins debating toward a more accurate estimation of story points for the user story.

Daily Scrum

Often referred to as *daily stand-ups*, these are short activities, usually of five to fifteen minutes, where the team shares the status of their activities (Figure 1-11).

Figure 1-11. *Sprint daily stand-ups*

A Scrum team is encouraged to have stand-ups every day; however, if the team is collaborative and communicative, you could have these activities happen every other day too (see Figure 1-12). The reference to stand-ups is because these meetings are short, and hence the team stands in formation to share their updates.

Sunday	Monday	Tuesday	Wednesday	Thursday
10 minutes daily stand-up		10 minutes daily stand-up		10 minutes daily stand-up
				sprint demo

Figure 1-12. *Sprint daily stand-up schedule*

The following are common updates to share with the team:

- Tasks you've completed yesterday or earlier this week
- Tasks you're working on and expect to complete today or until the next daily stand-up
- Challenges you're facing and possible risks you've identified

Sprint Demo

Referred to as the *sprint review* or *sprint demo*, this activity is held at the end or near the end of the sprint schedule, and its purpose is to demonstrate to the team and to the product owner the work done in the sprint and collect feedback from the Scrum team.

Sprint Retrospective

The sprint retrospective creates a medium to reflect on the work and processes of the sprint. It can be held within the sprint period, at the end, or sometime after. A common practice is also to hold release retrospectives.

Here are some general guidelines for conducting sprint retrospectives:

- *Recording items of things that went well*: This allows for promoting good feedback for team members and acknowledging good work that has been done and should be continued.
- *Recording items of things to improve*: This allows for providing constructive feedback on items that may need more attention and more refinement for future sprints to be more successful.
- *Creating action items*: This is to learn further for future improvement; it is required to create action items and assign them to team members.

Avoiding Agile Pitfalls

People react differently to change, so adopting new processes requires managing the change and following through with everyone patiently and gradually so that the change is introduced and embraced.

If your team didn't adopt an agile methodology before or has used a different one, the following key guidelines should help in adopting the Scrum agile methodology effectively with minimal risks:

- *Avoid excessive change adoption*: Avoid adapting Scrum altogether and, instead, from release to release try to adopt more Scrum guidelines and concepts. Making a change all at once often fails miserably, so take baby steps to integrate Scrum activities in your team.

- *Adopt what is right*: You may find that some Scrum guidelines, concepts, or activities are not working well for your team. If you tried it and you found it not to be working, don't force processes on your team. Instead, be flexible to embrace processes that do work.

- *Trust*: Scrum agile development methodology lies a lot on the trust in your team, whether it's breaking down features or estimating their scope. Embrace and encourage team members to be proactive.

- *Communicate*: One of the foundations of the agile philosophy is to encourage communication across your team, which should elevate team collaboration.

- *Get feedback*: Constructive feedback is crucial for continuous improvements in Scrum and one of the basic principles of it. Embrace feedback, but avoid good or bad excessive or exaggerated feedback.

- *Strive for automation*: You want test automation and build automation.

Summary

In this chapter, we reviewed agile software development through the origins of other models like Waterfall and various agile flavors. You then learned about the practices of agile Scrum and basic artifacts such as the product backlog, sprint backlog, and Scrum roles, and we explained the processes and activities held during sprints. We concluded this chapter by explaining how to avoid common pitfalls when introducing and practicing agile software development in order to adopt the process in a better and safe way.

CHAPTER 2

Getting Started with Agile Manager

In the previous chapter, you learned about the agile software development methodology and some concepts from this philosophy. To streamline the management of a software project's development life cycle, HP introduced Agile Manager (AGM).

In this chapter, you'll learn the basics of Agile Manager and how to get started with it if you haven't already. We'll cover the following topics:

- Introducing HP's Agile Manager

- Obtaining an account for Agile Manager

- Getting acquainted with the interface

Introducing HP's Agile Manager

HP isn't new to the market for software development life cycle (SDLC) applications for enterprises; it already has sustained a large market share thanks to its Quality Center application, which provides software requirements management, test management, and other software life-cycle capabilities. Quality Center serves as a component of HP's broader Application Lifecycle Management solution, which is for on-premise enterprise deployments. However, this traditional software offering isn't up-to-date with a modern web application's software as a service (SaaS) model, which gives customers quick access to service applications through the Web.

Note You can learn more about Application Lifecycle Management from HP at
`http://www8.hp.com/us/en/software-solutions/application-lifecycle-management.html`.

To catch up with the market for online agile project planning, HP introduced Agile Manager, which is an SaaS-based solution for managing the life cycle and delivery of software and which can also be deployed on-premise for enterprises that seek to contain their application life-cycle management in their own data center and off the cloud.

Agile Manager features a rich and modern web application by employing a single-page application architecture for an optimal native-application experience and offers other characteristics such as inline editing. One of its best strengths may be its multifaceted view for the overall software life cycle, enabling requirements management based on the agile philosophy of themes and features. Supporting build and automation processes through DevOps is also made possible through integration with tools such as Jenkins, Git, and more. All of this functionality is tunneled into a dashboard interface and multiple widgets, which can be customized, and Agile Manager provides the team leader or general management roles with clear visibility into the real-time status of current projects.

As of the writing of this book, the current Agile Manager version available for SaaS customers is 2.10.

15

Application Setup

Managing releases, sprints, and their teams is made simple through a toggle switch to the Agile Manager configuration mode. This mode enables easy planning and setup; Figure 2-1 shows a release details page.

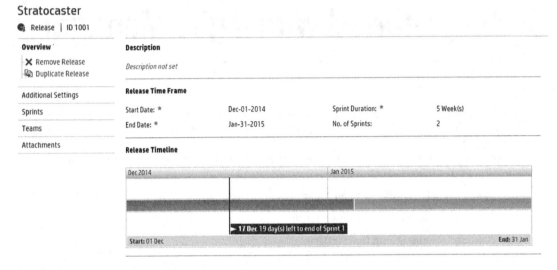

Figure 2-1. *Release details in configuration mode*

The application setup enables instant access to managing the workspace and insight into the release backlog via a calendar, which shows a Gantt-style representation of the planned sprints.

Release and Sprint Planning

Release and sprint planning are some of the most important tasks for any software manager to take on, and when working with Agile Manager, you'll find that the tool supports the process instead of forcing you to align with its own flow.

As you can see in Figure 2-2, the Sprint Backlog view is informative, providing not only sprint items such as user stories and defects but also statistics widgets at the top-right corner, including the schedule and time left for the current sprint. The Sprint Backlog view also provides a glimpse into each item's tasks and acceptance tests as well as member planning information. Furthermore, the grid layout listing can be customized to include more status and information fields for display.

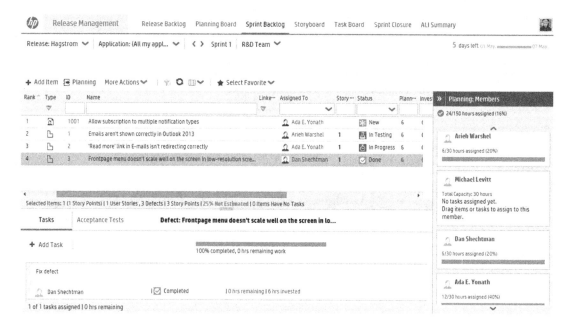

Figure 2-2. *Sprint Backlog view*

Kanban and Scrumban Storyboard

Whether you're a fan of the Scrum or Kanban methodology or you're the sophisticated team leader who chooses Scrumban to run your software development, Agile Manager will easily enable you to streamline the work process for any of these styles.

The Storyboard view, as shown in Figure 2-3, lists sprint backlog items per each lane: Planning, In Progress, and Done, by default. You can further customize and extend this view, and you can move items through the lanes by dragging and dropping, just like on a physical Scrum board.

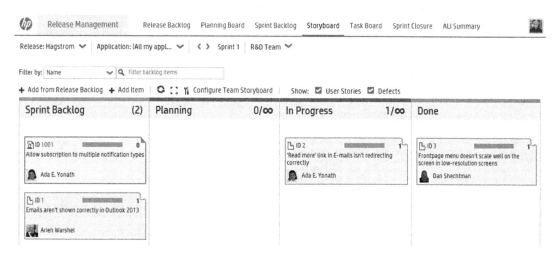

Figure 2-3. *Storyboard view*

Streamlining the Sprint Workflow

Another view that showcases the flexibility of Agile Manager is its Sprint Closure view, as shown in Figure 2-4. This view shows information and summaries that don't collide with the process and workflow that a team leader or manager may have chosen as the workflow. Items can be easily tracked in the future, and practical action items can be taken through user stories assignment for future releases.

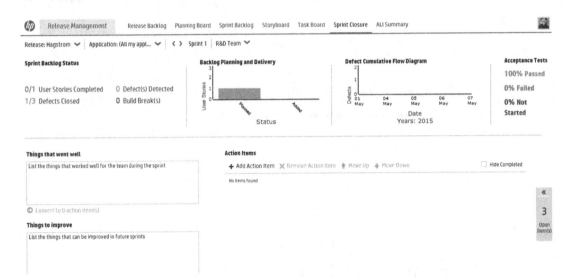

Figure 2-4. *Sprint Closure view*

Dashboard

In the fast-paced world of software development, it is essential to keep an eye on how development progresses, and Agile Manager's Dashboard view has been designed exactly for that, as shown in Figure 2-5. The contextual components feature enables you to quickly switch between the various teams, sprints, or applications and monitor their status as the widgets update in real time.

Figure 2-5. *Dashboard view*

Dashboard components are extremely customizable, and the view provides the ability to control and configure the column layout. It also supports a full-screen view so that dashboards can easily be projected on heads-up displays (HUDs).

Build and SCM Integration

Integrating build systems and source code management into life-cycle management allows for a much more detailed view and connected interface. This is even more true with the DevOps methodology that plays a key role in the software development life cycle, providing automatic actions such as referencing a defect ID in a developer's commit message that closes the defect and set its status to Fixed.

Having a connected hub of the entire software development life cycle, including the technical aspects of managing builds, provides an even clearer view for managers, who can pinpoint the exact change set or user stories development that resulted in a failed build process. It also provides valuable insight for the development team, which can easily identify and resolve issues.

Signing Up for HP's Agile Manager

As mentioned previously, HP's Agile Manager offers an SaaS-based solution for agile teams, startups, and companies or organizations that want to follow the SaaS-based pricing and on-the-go licensing model. Larger enterprises and companies that want to own Agile Manager in their own datacenters can deploy an on-premise Agile Manager solution as part of HP's application life-cycle management solution.

SaaS-Based Agile Manager

Browse to www.hp.com/go/agilemanager, as shown in Figure 2-6, and click the Try Me button to begin the sign-up process for the SaaS-based solution. HP provides a limited-time trial edition that users can experiment with, so we will use that for this book; later you are welcome to extend it. The free trial edition is a 30-day fully featured Agile Manager instance and allows you to configure up to ten users for managing and participating in the Agile Manager application.

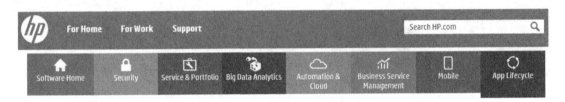

AGILE MANAGER

SaaS-based Agile project management solution to organize, plan, and execute Agile projects. Leverages native cloud architecture for instant-on access, boasts a clean, intuitive design, removes latencies, bolsters Agile practices, and fosters continuous improvement.

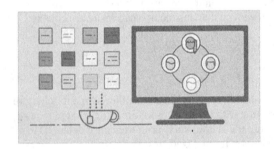

A Lean, Mean, Agile Machine

HP Agile Manager unites your teams by providing real-time, 360-degree visibility into tasks, metrics and progress. Remove latencies, bolster agile practices and foster continuous improvement.

Try Me

Figure 2-6. *Agile Manager official web site*

Once you have clicked the Try Me or Free Trial buttons available on the web page, you'll be redirected to signing up, as shown in Figure 2-7.

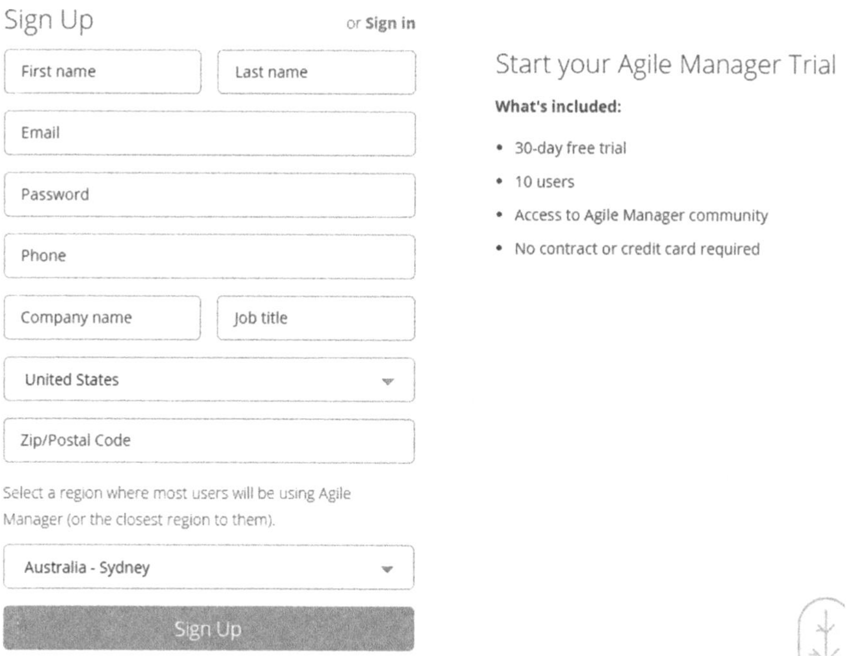

Sign Up

or **Sign in**

First name

Last name

Email

Password

Phone

Company name

Job title

United States ▾

Zip/Postal Code

Select a region where most users will be using Agile
Manager (or the closest region to them).

Australia - Sydney ▾

Sign Up

Start your Agile Manager Trial

What's included:

- 30-day free trial
- 10 users
- Access to Agile Manager community
- No contract or credit card required

Figure 2-7. *Agile Manager registration page*

Fill in your details in the sign-up form, and within a minute you should receive an e-mail in your inbox to activate your free trial edition. Follow the link in the e-mail, and you'll be presented with the page for beginning the trial period, as shown in Figure 2-8.

Start your Agile Manager Trial

What's included:

- 30-day free trial
- 10 users
- Access to Agile Manager community
- No contract or credit card required

Select a region where most users will be using Agile Manager (or the closest region to them).

Figure 2-8. *Agile Manager trial page*

Click Next, and then your account will be signed up with an Agile Manager instance. On the next page, simply click the Go To My Account button, and you'll be redirected into the HP SaaS platform, as shown in Figure 2-9, which provides access to Agile Manager. Within a minute, the Agile Manager instance should be ready, and you should see it listed on the products page.

Figure 2-9. *Agile Manager account page*

To begin working with Agile Manager for the first time, click the Launch button to the right of the page, and the application will start loading.

■ **Note** When visiting the HP SaaS platform for Agile Manager web page for the first time, you'll be presented with a Getting Started wizard that introduces you to the platform for Agile Manager and several key areas, such as user management, the products page, how to get support, and how to configure your account settings. Agile Manager will also present pop-ups of new features as they are released, from time to time.

The welcome page for the Agile Manager application will greet you with helpful information and videos for getting started, as shown in Figure 2-10. To continue, click the Getting Started button at the bottom of the page.

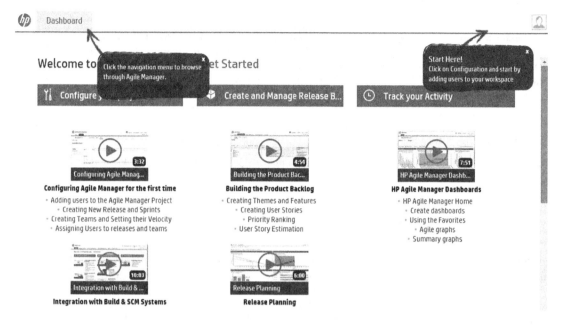

Figure 2-10. Agile Manager welcome page

Getting Acquainted with Agile Manager

To get you started with Agile Manager, we will walk you through the key parts and navigation areas of the user interface. We will focus on the navigation menu, getting you familiar with the main grid area and general working area.

As we mentioned, Agile Manager was created based on modern web technologies, ensuring an improved user experience (UX). To provide users with the best possible application experience, it was built on a single-page application architecture, and thus the navigation and usage will feel much like a native desktop application.

When you log in to Agile Manager for the first time, you will notice that it takes a few seconds to load, which is common with single-page applications because they download some data from the server and into your browser to maintain the native-application experience. Once that's done, you're ready to begin exploring Agile Manager.

Navigation Menu

The top navigation area makes it possible to browse the main activities when working on your agile projects. The menu splits into categories as denoted in the gray rectangle and provides access to the Dashboard, Product Backlog, Release Management, Defect Management, Builds, and Source Code views. Upon selecting any of these main areas, the submenu will update to the relevant navigation items. For example, when selecting Release Management, the submenu will update to include pages such as Release Backlog, Planning Board, Sprint Backlog, and others (see Figure 2-11).

Figure 2-11. Navigation menu, Release Management selected

On the left side of the navigation area you will find quick access to your account personalization settings, which will show up with your name and avatar. The next item will be the workspace name, which denotes the current AGM tenant account being used (you'll learn more about workspaces later in the book). This is followed by a gear icon that switches between the application mode and the configuration area. Finally, you will find icons for accessing various support channels and logging out of your account sessions.

■ **Note**   When using Agile Manager, you won't need to use your browser's built-in support for going back and forth in page history; rather, you should be using AGM's navigation menu and thus avoid unnecessary complete-page reloads.

Contextual Filters

In almost every page and section of Agile Manager, you will find contextual filters that are used to better align the page view, widgets, and overall information on the screen with the correct context.

Figure 2-12 shows one of these contextual filters on the Release Management ➤ Release Backlog page, which shows the release content. Switching between different releases—past, present, and future—is easy by simply selecting from the available options in the release filter that shows up under the navigation menu. This page further provides the ability to filter by the application that the release is associated with, where you may choose one, few, or none to avoid any filtering altogether.

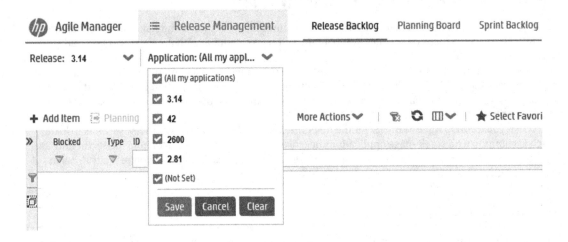

Figure 2-12. Contextual filters

Page Widgets

Just like with contextual filters, you will often find varying widgets on pages, in the top-right area, to indicate status or summarize the current information that is being viewed.

For example, if you navigate to Release Management ➤ Sprint Backlog to view the status of the sprint, you'll notice that the widgets will provide an overall update as to the timeline of the sprint, with an indication of the number of days remaining for the sprint (if it is the current sprint), the ending date, and the current date. Other widgets also feature a backlog status, as shown in Figure 2-13, that displays a visual representation of the sprint items broken down by their status (New, In Progress, In Testing, and Done), as well as the Task Summary widgets, showing similar visual representation.

Figure 2-13. *Status widgets*

Similar to contextual filters, page widgets will show different information and a different set of widgets in each page, as relevant.

The Grid

Most of the work you'll be doing in Agile Manager is through the grid, which is a table-layout interface for managing and viewing data. In most pages, the grid, as shown in Figure 2-14, will consist of the following parts:

- *Toolbar*: The grid layout includes a toolbar to manage the items in the table, such as moving items to different releases or sprints, sending items by e-mail, or updating items. Other buttons on the grid help organize the table layout such as clearing any filters set on the table, reloading the data to refresh the items list, and setting relevant columns to display.

- *Left panel sidebar*: The panel on the left of the grid sidebar is used to apply or revoke formatting on the table layout in terms of managing filters and grouping items based on their properties to create a collapsible list.

- *Right panel sidebar*: To the right of the table you'll mostly find helpful data organization tools such as team buckets when viewing the release backlog or member buckets when viewing the sprint backlog. Similar tools such as defects buckets show up on the defects view, and so on. You will often find these buckets and planning tools helpful to use because you can easily drag and drop items from the grid straight into items in the buckets on the right panel.

- *Grid items*: The primary content of the grid is the items listing, which shows up in a column-based table layout. The table features sortable columns for basic ascending and descending sorting, as well as more advanced sorting such as date ranges for item properties like Creation Date, Detected by, Fixed on Date, and so on. The columns are also draggable and allow for quick ordering of the table as well as enabling filter capabilities by most of the structured properties.

- *Bottom panel*: On most pages, like Release Backlog, the bottom panel features a minimal status information block that is interactive, so clicking some of its text links will allow you to toggle between different status options. On other pages, such as Sprint Backlog, the bottom panel features a more in-depth panel that will show extra metadata on each item, once an item is selected from the layout. An example of this extra metadata is a user story's tasks list and acceptance tests.

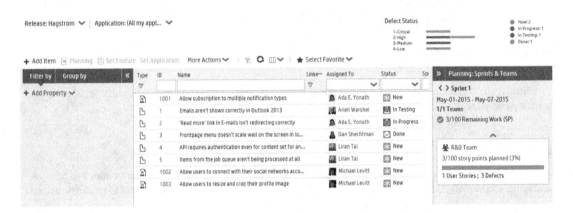

Figure 2-14. *Grid layout*

Item Page

The grid layout listing, backlog list, and all visual representation widgets are composed of *items*, whether these are defects, user stories, or other types such as configuration items. So far, you've seen how items are managed and viewed as an aggregated list, but items are created initially with minimal data and then are updated with their entire properties set. Each item, such as defect, user story, or feature, has its own item page view, as shown in Figure 2-15 for defects.

'Read more' link in E-mails isn't redirecting correctly

⌐ Defect | ID 2

Overview	Details				Related People	
✉ Send by E-Mail	Defect Status: *	⊙ Open	Severity: *	▥ 2-High	Detected By: *	🔲 Liran Tal
	Modified:	Dec-18-2014 04:53:15	Detected in Release:	Hagstrom	Assigned To:	🔴 Ada E. Yonath
Linked Items	Detected on Date: *	Dec-18-2014	Closed on Date:	*No value*		
Attachments	Fixed on Date:	*No value*	Priority:	*No value*	**Attachments**	
History	Show More...				*Drop Here*	📎
Development Activity					No attachments	

Release Plan

Theme:		Subscriptions	Application:	Messaging and Notif...
Feature :		Allow users to subsc...	Release:	Hagstrom
Sprint:		Sprint 1	Team:	R&D Team
Story Points:		1	Status: *	⊙ In Progress
Blocked Item:		⊖ Not Blocked	Click to block item	

Linked Items
No linked items

Planned vs. Actual (Hours)
0 ──── 5 ──── 10

Comments (0) 💬 Add Comment

Related Tasks (1) ✛ Add Task
33% completed, 6 hrs remaining work

Development Metrics

Code Changes
0 lines   0 files
Metrics source is missing.

Figure 2-15. *Defect item page*

Whether the item is a defect or a user story, it will mostly benefit from the same set of features and properties as well as the same user interface, yet some fields vary because of the characteristics of the items.

- *Left sidebar panel*: This accordion-style layout panel features a more focused navigation area for the item data, such as the detailed overall overview and quick access to Linked Items, Attachments, History, and Development Activity views (only where source code management integration is applicable).

- *The main content area*: The center area will feature most of your day-to-day work when working with backlog items. In this area you will be providing descriptions and setting important properties such as defect status, severity, feature, story points, and so on. The tasks interface allows you to record a task list for both defects and user stories and enables tracking tasks through an hour-based time measure as well as tasks status option. Once updated, the tasks update all the item's status properties accordingly. Collaboration on backlog items is made possible through the commenting system, which every item has, and through the availability to share items via the Send by E-mail action.

- *Right sidebar panel*: At the right of any backlog item you can find general information such as the related people; this includes mainly the author of the item and the person the item is assigned to. Other information blocks you can find quick access to are attachments and linked items, and you easily tell the progress of the item based on the visualization of the Planned vs. Actual widget.

Configuration Mode

When we covered the navigation menu earlier, we noted the gray gear icon on the right side of the top navigation menu. Clicking this icon toggles between the configuration mode and Agile Manager's application mode.

Within the configuration mode, shown in Figure 2-16, the following areas are available to set up:

- *Site*: This allows you to configure sitewide properties such as creating workspaces, which are instances of an AGM application, thus allowing one tenant to manage multiple, isolated projects with a single Agile Manager account. The Site area also allows you to add customizable properties on backlog items, as well as setting up the user accounts access to Agile Manager, including roles management and more.

- *Workspace*: In the Workspace configuration area, you can set up the current Agile Manager project instance settings and its defaults. For example, you can set defaults for story points and time estimation on user stories and tasks. You can also set up the source code management integration with AGM and applications that you want to track with AGM. Setting up the release information also takes place in the Workspace ➤ Releases management area, where you can set up the release timeline, create sprints, and build the teams.

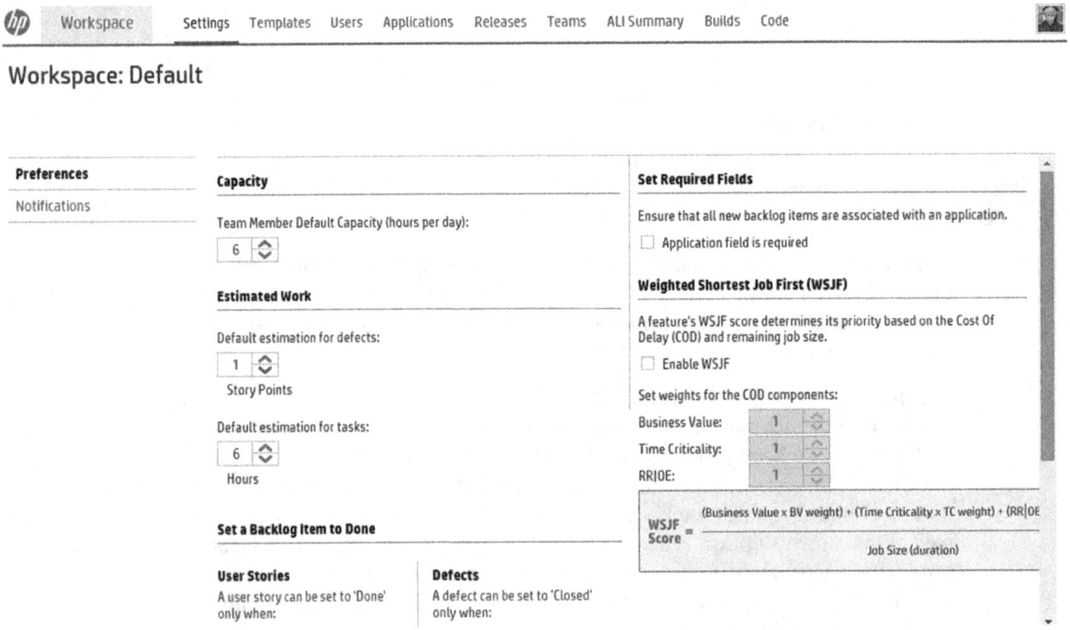

Figure 2-16. *Configuration mode*

Summary

In this chapter, you learned about the basics of Agile Manager and its origins as part of HP Software's application life-cycle management portfolio. You also learned how to sign up for an Agile Manager account on the cloud, through HP's SaaS offering. We also walked you through Agile Manager's user interface and the various screens and onscreen widgets it supports so you could get acquainted with it.

CHAPTER 3

Setting Up Agile Manager for Release

In the previous chapter, you learned about Agile Manager's origins and got acquainted with its capabilities and user interface. You also explored the various pages and screen components that make up for the navigation and page information. You also signed up for a trial Agile Manager account on HP's software as a service (SaaS) cloud to begin working on your agile software project.

In this chapter, you'll learn how to set up an Agile Manager account so that you can prepare all that is required to begin managing releases. In specific, we will cover the following topics:

- Setting up custom variables and workspaces and managing users

- Workspace administration for customized default options, backlog items templates, and mail notification events

- Creating a release and planning the sprints and teams accordingly

Setting Up a Site

To begin working in the configuration area, you need to toggle to configuration mode first. Click the gray gear icon to the right of the top navigation area, as shown in Figure 3-1.

Figure 3-1. Configuration toggle

Once you have switched to the configuration mode, the navigation area will change accordingly to reflect this change by replacing the *Agile Manager* text to the right of the configuration page with *Agile Manager Configuration* as well as enhancing the gray gear icon with an arrow pointing to the left, as shown in Figure 3-2.

Figure 3-2. Configuration mode

You're now ready to continue working in the configuration mode to begin setting up your site.

Managing Workspaces

The first tab in the Site area is the Workspaces, as shown in Figure 3-3, which enables an Agile Manager user account to open and create several working instances of Agile Manager, called *workspaces*. Even though the workspaces are using their own applications, themes, and features, they still share the same sitewide settings such as custom variables, and they may share the same users as well.

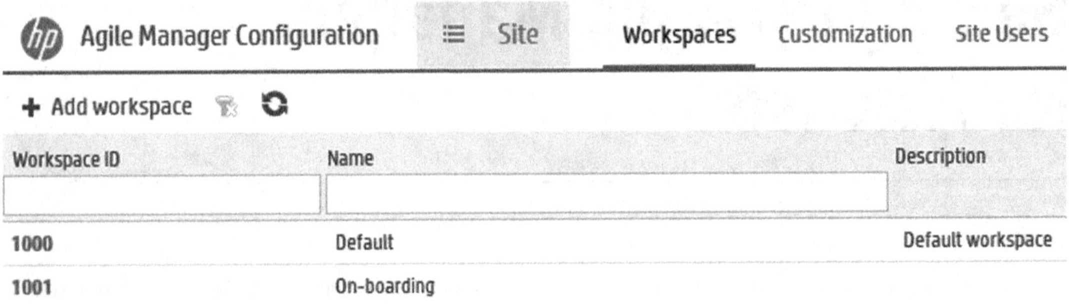

Workspace ID	Name	Description
1000	Default	Default workspace
1001	On-boarding	

Figure 3-3. Workspaces configuration

■ **Note** Agile Manager supports different user roles, such as an application administrator and a viewer. Users who were added and set as nonworkspace administrators will not be able to access the configuration area.

You can think of a workspace as an Agile Manager tenant-based account, which is able to manage several projects with just one account. All Agile Manager sites include a default workspace named Default, and any accounts are assigned there, unless otherwise defined.

■ **Note** By default, Agile Manager allows you to create up to 10 workspaces. If you require more, you should explore the option of upgrading your Agile Manager account.

Customizing Fields

Like with most tools and applications you use, you'll probably want to customize the fields for an item such as a user story or a defect or even add your own fields. Agile Manager allows you to do that for the following backlog items: themes, features, user stories, and defects.

■ **Note** For each backlog item type, Agile Manager allows you to add up to five custom fields.

Let's extend the Agile Manager instance by creating some customized fields for some of the backlog item types. Navigate to Site area and then click the Custom Fields tab. This will open a similar page to the one shown in Figure 3-4, which already includes some custom fields defined.

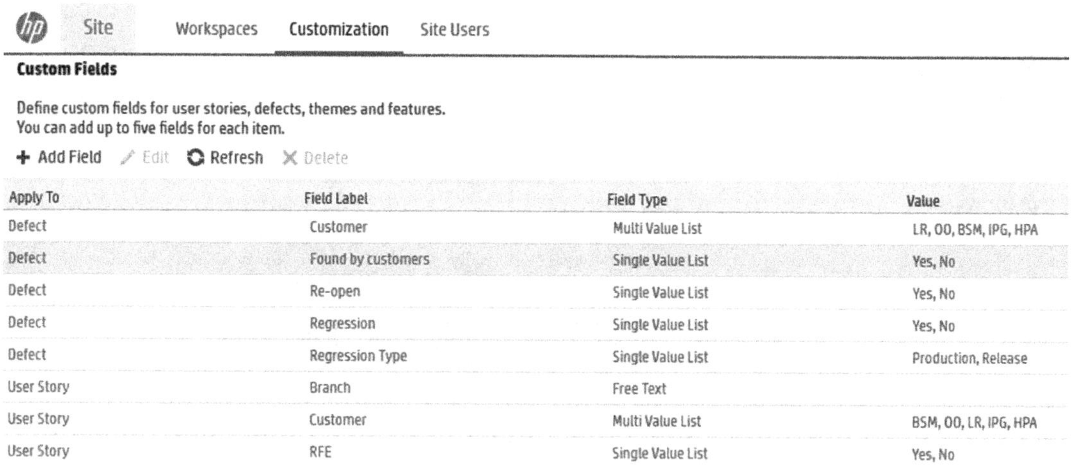

	Site	Workspaces	Customization	Site Users

Custom Fields

Define custom fields for user stories, defects, themes and features.
You can add up to five fields for each item.

+ Add Field ✎ Edit **↻ Refresh** ✕ Delete

Apply To	Field Label	Field Type	Value
Defect	Customer	Multi Value List	LR, OO, BSM, IPG, HPA
Defect	Found by customers	Single Value List	Yes, No
Defect	Re-open	Single Value List	Yes, No
Defect	Regression	Single Value List	Yes, No
Defect	Regression Type	Single Value List	Production, Release
User Story	Branch	Free Text	
User Story	Customer	Multi Value List	BSM, OO, LR, IPG, HPA
User Story	RFE	Single Value List	Yes, No

Figure 3-4. *Custom fields configuration*

Here, you can see a similar view of the grid you saw in Chapter 2. The grid allows to sort by the Apply To field only, and the toolbar options enable the fields management, such as Add Field, Edit, and Delete.

Managing Custom Fields

Next, click the Add Field option on the top left of the toolbar, and the Add Field pop-up will display, as shown in Figure 3-5. You'll add a custom field now: enter **branch** as the Field Label value and set its Apply To value to User Story for that specific backlog item type, in which you will store the Git branch name (or any other source code management solution you're using) where the user story is developed on. Because the branch name can be any sort of string, let's define the Field Type to be Free Text.

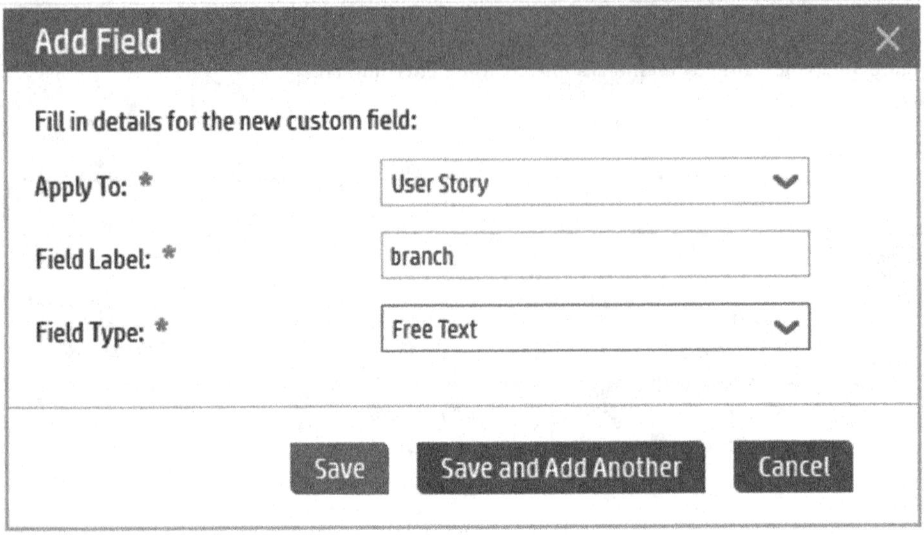

Figure 3-5. *Adding custom field*

Now click the Save and Add Another button. Let's add another type of field that allows you to record production-related bugs. In the new Add Field dialog, set the Apply To value to Defect, enter **Production** for its Field Label value, and set the Field Type value to Single Value List. To the Field Values list, add Yes and No options, and click Save to finish. This field will enable you to track bugs in production that you consider critical and must go through hot-fix mode because they are affecting customers on a live system.

■ **Note** You're welcome to experiment with more field types such as the Multi Value List, which allows you to define a customer list and select more than one option; this can be used to specify the customers affected by a defect.

After adding fields, it won't be possible to change their field types or the backlog item type they apply to. Editing an existing field, as shown in Figure 3-6, allows you to change only the label for the field, so think carefully before massively utilizing a field in a backlog item.

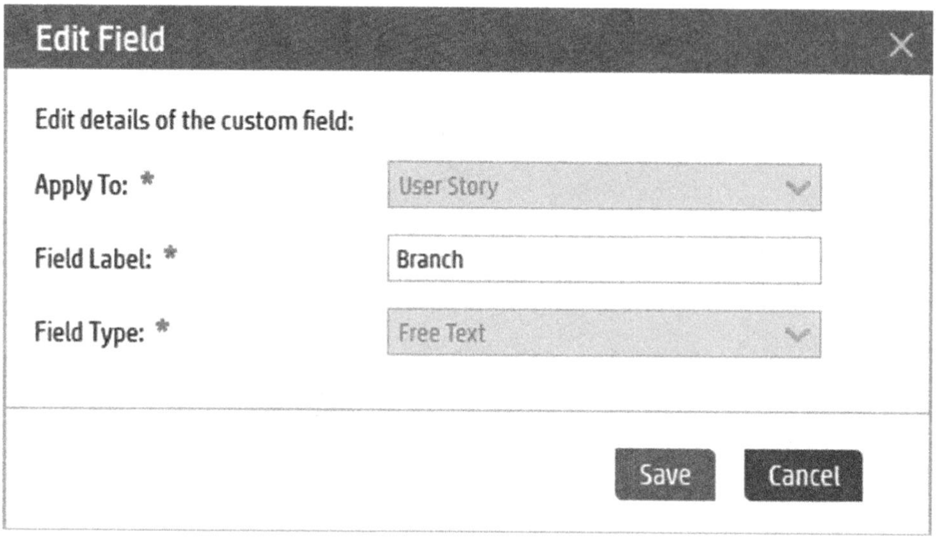

Edit Field   ✕

Edit details of the custom field:

Apply To: *   User Story   ⌄

Field Label: *   Branch

Field Type: *   Free Text   ⌄

                                        Save   Cancel

Figure 3-6. *Editing custom field*

■ **Note**   When adding custom fields, it's a good practice to test them in a few places before massively utilizing them across the project or the entire group. For example, try to filter, group, and create dashboards based on these fields and see whether they bring in any value with the field setup you used, or maybe you need to assign this field to another backlog item type.

Tracking Custom Fields

Agile Manager allows you to track custom fields, up to three, for each backlog item type. Tracking these fields will enable you to create widgets for the dashboard to view them in historical representation and see how that field changed.

To enable tracking, navigate to Site ➤ Custom Fields, locate the field, right-click to display the pop-up options, and choose Edit (or simply select the item from the grid rows and click the Edit option in the grid toolbar) to display the Edit Field pop-up page, as shown in Figure 3-7.

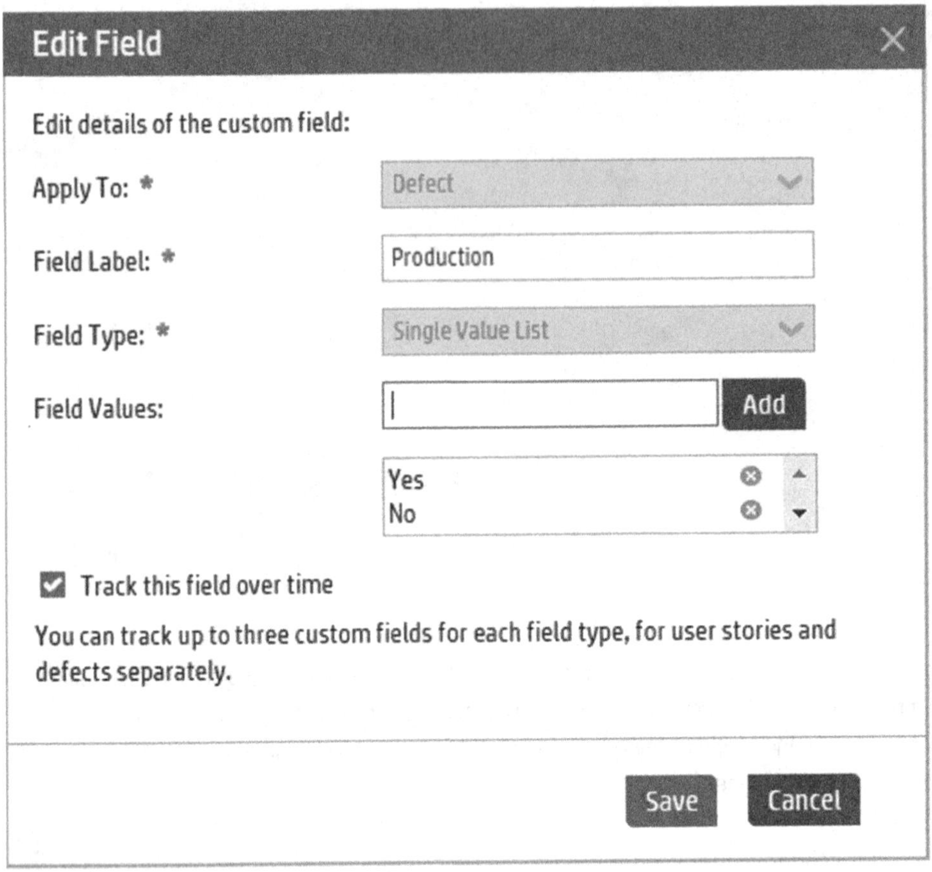

Figure 3-7. *Tracking custom field*

Once there, toggle the "Track this field over time" option and click Save.

Setting Up Users

To begin working with Agile Manager in your team, you need to begin creating users so team members can log in and participate in the agile project you'll be managing.

You set up user accounts via a grid layout, which by default lists all existing user accounts, their status, their contact information, and their roles in assigned workspaces (see Figure 3-8). This page also includes a widget in the top-right corner to provide information for site administrators on the number of licenses in use and remaining for user accounts.

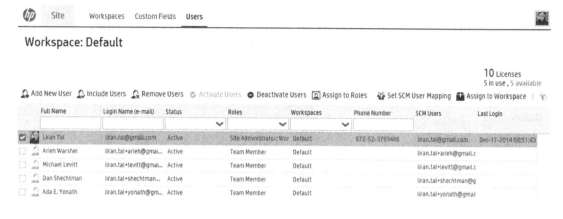

Figure 3-8. *Users setup grid*

When adding users, note that it is possible to create accounts for them only if their e-mail address is in the same domain as the Agile Manager admin user account or if their e-mail domain is listed in your account's trusted domains settings.

■ **Note** If you need to add another domain under your account, it's necessary to contact Agile Manager's support team to configure this setting. You'll learn more about contacting support in Chapter 7.

To begin adding your team members to Agile Manager, navigate to Site ➤ Users, as shown in Figure 3-8, and click Add New User in the grid toolbar. In the Add New User pop-up, as shown in Figure 3-9, you should fill in all of the account information such as the login name, which expects an e-mail address; the team member's name; and a phone number for additional contact information. If you are going to manage more than a single instance of Agile Manager, then you can choose to assign the user to its relevant workspace; otherwise, the default option is good to proceed with and represents the current workspace. If the user is expected to be an administrator of the workspace, you can assign the Workspace Administrator role; otherwise, choosing the default Team Member option is good as the default.

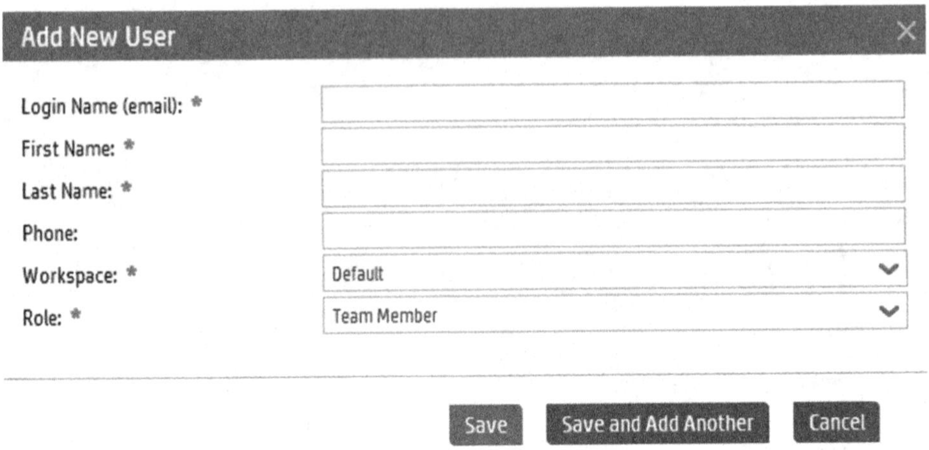

Figure 3-9. *Creating new user*

Users can't be edited in the grid area once they are added, and you would need to remove the user and re-add it with the right information if you made a mistake when populating this data in the pop-up. Users themselves, though, are able to change their contact information and even upload a picture, but changing an e-mail address remains impossible and would require you to re-create the user.

To remove users, simply toggle them on in the grid layout and click the Remove Users option, which will allow you to confirm or reject the action.

■ **Note** If users were previously active in Agile Manager (in other words, they created backlog items or were assigned to items), then their items will continue to exist and won't be removed, and their reference will be a nonlinkable username in the form of e-mail address so they can be still identified, even though their account was removed.

Moreover, users who were removed from the Agile Manager application instance will still exist as their original account in HP SaaS solution. To completely remove these users, they should be removed from the SaaS account too.

To temporarily disable users, you can use the Deactivate Users option from the grid toolbar (and its corresponding Activate Users option to reenable them), all without entirely removing the user.

Let's review more options on the grid toolbar.

- *Assign to Roles*: This allows you to assign the toggled users to different roles. Keep in mind that the Site Administrator role is quite powerful and includes the tasks of creating workspaces and configuring sitewide settings, so it should be granted with care. Workspace Administrator can only manage the current workspace, and Team Member is a fully functional member account to use Agile Manager. The ALI Dev Bridge role is used to integrate AGM with your source code management system and may not be used to access AGM itself through the web interface. A quick method to grant or revoke roles to a specific user is to double-click the Roles column in the grid, which will open the roles management pop-up.

- *Set SCM User Mapping*: When integrating Agile Manager with a source code management system, it is required to map Agile Manager users with the authors of code commits. To create this mapping, AGM allows you to configure the e-mail addresses of commit authors for team member accounts.

- *Assign to Workspace*: This allows you to assign a user to any workspaces created on the Agile Manager site instance.

Setting Up a Workspace

The Workspace configuration area allows you to set the current workspace settings and adjust the behavior as desired. More than just setting up configuration parameters, it actually allows you to streamline the workflow. For example, a Workspace Administrator can decide that a defect can't be changed to a Done status unless it has passed a predefined value of success rate for unit tests.

Workspace Preferences

To begin setting up the workspace settings, as shown in Figure 3-10, navigate to Workspace ➤ Settings, which loads the Preferences subtab in the left navigation panel; we'll review some of the most commonly used options.

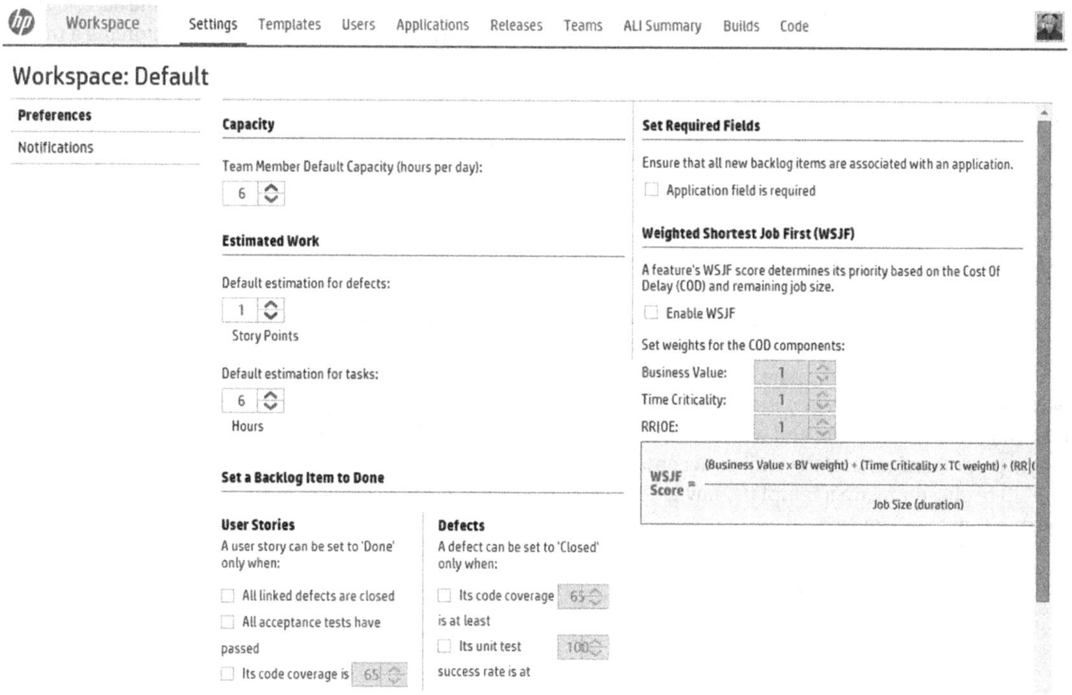

Figure 3-10. *Workspace settings*

Capacity

In the Capacity configuration section, you can set the default effort capacity for users in releases. The capacity is measured in hours per day and can be overridden for each member individually within each release.

Work Estimation Defaults

In the Estimated Work configuration section, AGM can automatically populate backlog items with default estimations when they are initially created. You will later see how you can also create default tasks and other properties for backlog items.

By setting the Story Points on the "Default estimation for defects" option, new defects that get created will have the chosen Story Points value already set. By setting the time value in hours on the "Default estimation for tasks" option, tasks created on user stories or defects will be populated with a default time value set as selected for this option.

Controlling Done Status

In the Set a Backlog Item to Done configuration section, it is possible to control whether a defect or user story will be allowed to change its status to Done, based on predefined rules criteria.

Agile Manager allows you to link backlog items one to another, which is useful for creating a rule that defines that a user story is allowed to be set to the Done status only when all of its linked defects are closed. To enable that rule, simply toggle on the "All linked defects are closed" option. Similarly, you can define acceptance tests for user stories, and by toggling on the "All acceptance tests have passed" option, you'll be enforcing a rule where all acceptance tests must be set to Passed status for the user story to change its status to Done.

Defects and user stories share another rule criteria, which can be set on both to enforce the Done status change, based on code quality. By setting the values for both options to "Its code coverage is at least" and "Its unit test success rate is at least," it is possible to rely on Agile Manager integration with automated build tools like Jenkins.

Workspace Templates

Workspace templates further build on the work estimation defaults that you saw earlier on the Preferences tab by providing predefined options that are already populated and created on backlog item types.

With a workspace template, it is possible to define a workflow where for every new defect created, a task will be created, and even the default effort estimation for defects in story points will be assigned. Each task will use a specific title and will have a default time estimation for it. Similarly, with user stories, you can create predefined task sets as well as acceptance criteria.

To begin setting up a template, navigate to Workspace ➤ Templates, which will show a view similar to the one shown in Figure 3-11.

Workspace: Default

Create predefined templates to use when creating new user stories and defects. Create up to 5 templates for each backlog item type.

＋ Add Template   ⎘ Duplicate Template   ✕ Delete

🔍 Search template		Template Na...	User Story template		Item Type:	User Story ▾
User Stories	Defects	Modified:	🖼 liran.tal@gmail.com Dec-17-2014 19:29:07		Created:	🖼 liran.tal@gmail.com Dec-17-2014 19:29:07
User Story template ★		Template De...				

☑ Set as Default User Story Template

The following name, tasks, and acceptance criteria will be added to all user stories created using this template:

Story Name:

| General | Tasks | Acceptance Criteria |

＋ Add Tasks

Create unit tests

6 hrs estimated

Figure 3-11. *Workspace templates*

By default, Agile Manager should include a template for the Defects backlog item, so if you click Defects in the templates list, you should see a template called Default Defect Template, which includes one task titled "Fix defect," which is allotted six hours for the task time.

To add a new template for user stories, click User Stories in the templates list to switch to the templates for user stories and then click Add Template in the toolbar. A new template will be created in the right side of the template area, and you can now customize it. Set the template name to "User Story template." The Item Type field should be set to the User Story option. Select the option Set as Default User Story Template to make sure all newly created user stories will use this template. As an indication of the default template that was set, the template entry will feature a star to its right in the templates list.

To make the template more meaningful, you'll also add some tasks and acceptance tests for it. To begin with tasks, click the Tasks tab in the template that was added and then click Add Tasks, which will show the Add Task Template pop-up. To describe the task, enter some text, such as **Create unit tests**. Set the estimated hours and task color; click Add Another for more tasks to add to the template or click Save to finish. You can also switch to the Acceptance Criteria tab and add some acceptance tests as part of the template. When you're done, don't forget to click Save on the bottom sliding tab for the complete template to be saved.

■ **Note**   At the time of writing this book, each backlog item type can have up to five templates.

The templates management toolbar allows for more actions.

- *Duplicate Template*: If you'd like to create clones of some of your templates, defects, or user stories, you can just click this option and continue modifying the duplicated template.

- *Delete*: This option removes an existing template.

- *Import Template*: Users whom are able to access multiple workspaces will see this option in the toolbar; it will enable them to import a template that is used in another workspace into the current workspace.

Workspace Notifications

Agile Manager helps make communication effective by enabling e-mail notifications on specific events. Notifications are based on a few trigger rules only, which is good because it makes AGM less of a spammer.

Setting up workspace notifications is straightforward, as shown in Figure 3-12; nonetheless, it's an important task to do. To begin, navigate to Workspace ➤ Settings and click the Notifications tab on the left panel.

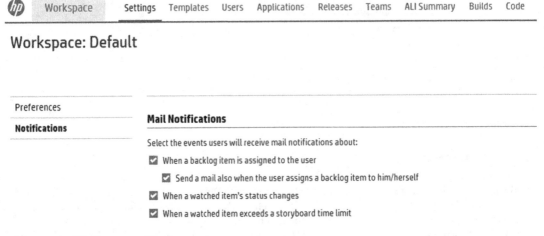

Figure 3-12. *Workspace notifications*

E-mail notifications will trigger when one of the toggled rules takes places. Agile Manager also provides a way to subscribe to notifications on a backlog item by toggling on its Watched status. Based on either of the predefined rules, the following notifications are provided:

- *Backlog item is assigned to the user*: Usually when backlog items are created, they aren't assigned to anyone specific, or they are manually assigned to a team leader or a generic user decided upon previously and are then later re-assigned correctly to a specific engineer. Upon every change of the assignee, Agile Manager will trigger a notification with the backlog item details.

- *Watched item is changing its status*: Another useful e-mail trigger rule happens when the backlog item's status is changed. This may often happen as defects move to In-Testing for QA or when they are re-opened because of regressions or issues with fixing a defect; this happens by setting the defect status to New or In-Progress again. Doing so will trigger a notification for you if you decided to watch the item.

- *Watched item exceeds a storyboard time limit*: When working with the Kanban-style storyboard interface, users can get notification when their watched items are exceeding the time limit, which was set for each lane in the storyboard. It is a good way to track status and make sure your team isn't late delivering.

We recommend toggling on all trigger rules and can assure you that your Agile Manager users will probably find it helpful.

As shown in Figure 3-13, e-mails that arrive in your inbox include quite useful information, such as the following:

- *Title*: Along with providing the backlog item ID, the title is a link to Agile Manager to open the backlog item quickly in your default web browser from your inbox.

- *Backlog item fields*: E-mails include fields that were deemed important by the Agile Manager team, such as the status field, severity, the release, the sprint the item is assigned to, and more.

- *Comments*: Any comments that were added on the backlog item are displayed to provide a discussion tree and visibility on this defect's history of communication.

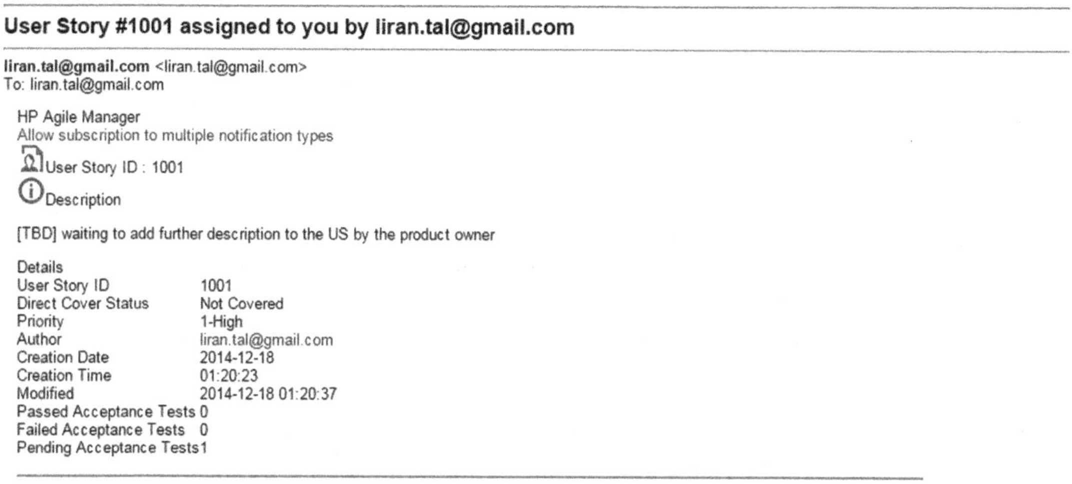

User Story #1001 assigned to you by liran.tal@gmail.com

---

liran.tal@gmail.com <liran.tal@gmail.com>
To: liran.tal@gmail.com

HP Agile Manager
Allow subscription to multiple notification types

User Story ID : 1001

Description

[TBD] waiting to add further description to the US by the product owner

Details
User Story ID   1001
Direct Cover Status   Not Covered
Priority   1-High
Author   liran.tal@gmail.com
Creation Date   2014-12-18
Creation Time   01:20:23
Modified   2014-12-18 01:20:37
Passed Acceptance Tests 0
Failed Acceptance Tests 0
Pending Acceptance Tests 1

Figure 3-13. *Workspace notifications example*

You'll learn later in the book how it is possible to manually trigger e-mail notifications in order to alert another user.

Workspace Applications

To begin managing applications that will be associated with backlog items, navigate to Workspace ➤ Applications, which will display the list of applications created in this workspace using the grid layout, as shown in Figure 3-14.

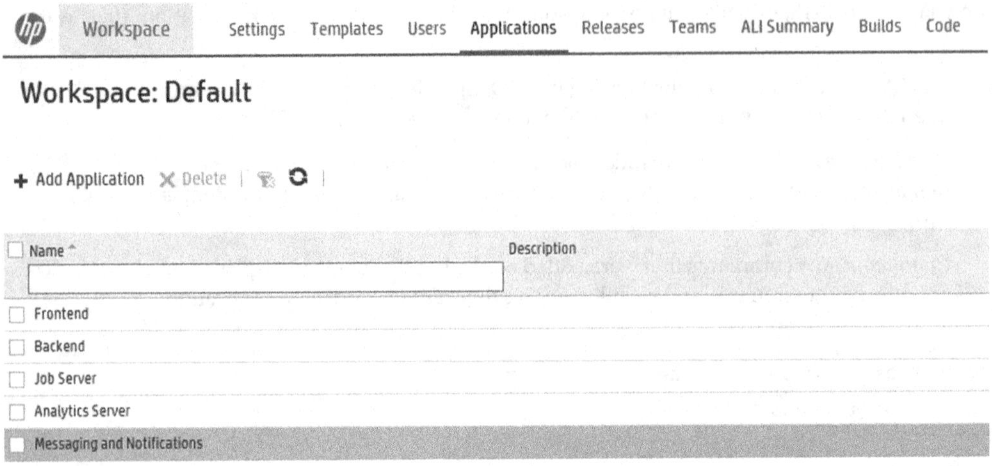

Figure 3-14. *Workspace applications*

Applications can be seen as various components that your product is separated into. These can be architectural components or functional components; any separation that works best for your agile project is suitable. The following are examples of applications:

- Front-end or back-end applications

- Web applications, notification systems, job servers, analytics servers

When applications are configured, they can be assigned to any of the following backlog items: themes, features, user stories, and defects; themes and features can be assigned multiple applications, thus allowing a feature that spans multiple applications to be associated with all of them.

■ **Note** When user stories or defects are associated with an application, their parents' feature and theme will be associated with that application as well. If, on the other hand, the application is left empty, then accordingly the backlog item will show "not set" on the application field.

Managing Applications

The grid view provides a simple management interface for setting up applications. Let's begin by adding an application, which is a fairly simple task. Click Add Application in the grid toolbar and fill in the fields for the application's name and description, as shown in Figure 3-15. Then either click Save to finish or continue to add more applications.

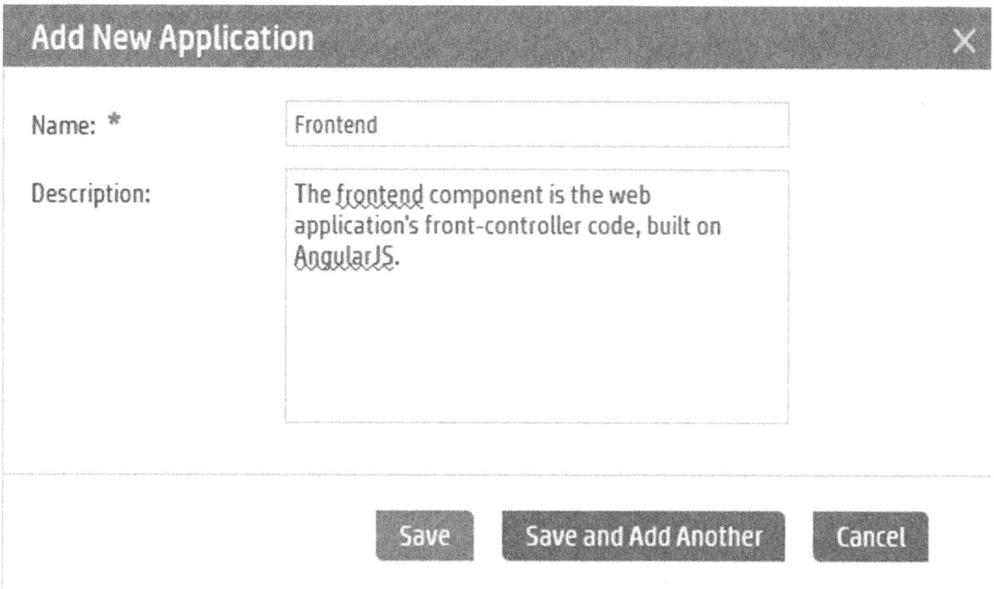

Add New Application ✕

Name: *   Frontend

Description: The frontend component is the web
                 application's front-controller code, built on
                 AngularJS.

Save   Save and Add Another   Cancel

Figure 3-15. Add New Application form

Deleting applications is fairly simple, by either toggling a single application to select it or clicking the toggle for the Name column in the grid to select all applications and then just clicking the Delete option from the toolbar. To edit an existing application, simply double-click its name or description fields on the actual grid listing, and inline editing will show up and allow you to refine the text for both fields.

▪ **Note**   Users are assigned applications, and they are allowed access to view any backlog item that is associated with their applications. If a user is not allowed access to an application, then any backlog item associated with it will not be visible for that user.

Applications will become useful later when you begin using Agile Manager for release and sprint management because you will be able to filter by applications or group results by them.

Workspace Users

When we reviewed the Site ➤ Users area, we were referring to adding users to Agile Manager as an application access. You learned how to add users via their e-mail or import them from the customer portal if they were already set there. Because of Agile Manager's flexibility with tenant-based separation, it is possible to manage users in different workspaces. For example, if you're managing a large agile project where you will be managing more than just one workspace, then you'll probably have different users assigned to different projects. These varied workspaces can be different R&D groups within your organization that are working toward achieving a single release or product, and therefore the workspaces will have different sets of users.

As a workspace administrator, you'll be able to manage the users in your own workspace. The overall users management is quite similar to the Site ➤ Users area, with some additional functionality that allows you to set configuration options that are relevant for the specific workspace.

To begin managing your workspace users, navigate to Workspace ➤ Users, which will display the list of users assigned to the current workspace using the grid layout, as shown in Figure 3-16.

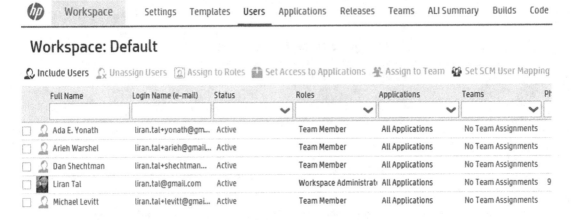

Figure 3-16. *Workspace users*

Since most of the user management functionality is similar to what was covered earlier in the general Site ➤ Users area, we'll be reviewing only the additional functionality here:

- *Include Users*: Allows a workspace administrator to add users to the current workspace from other workspaces

- *Unassign Users*: Removes the selected users from the current workspace

- *Set Access to Applications*: Selects which applications the selected users will have access to

- *Assign to Team*: Assigns the selected users to a specific team out of all releases and teams created

Setting Up the Release

Now that you have prepared the workspace settings and created your users, you can begin preparing the ground for your release, starting with the release setup. The release setup primarily includes defining the release timeline, the sprints, and the teams. Releases can also contain attachments such as technical specifications or design documents and may also be configured to work in either Scrum storyboard style or Kanban storyboard style, among other settings.

Figure 3-17 shows a release listing. To begin setting up the release, navigate to the Workspace ➤ Releases in the main navigation menu; either you will see the release details for a release that you last visited or you will see an empty release listing, which will prompt you to create a new release.

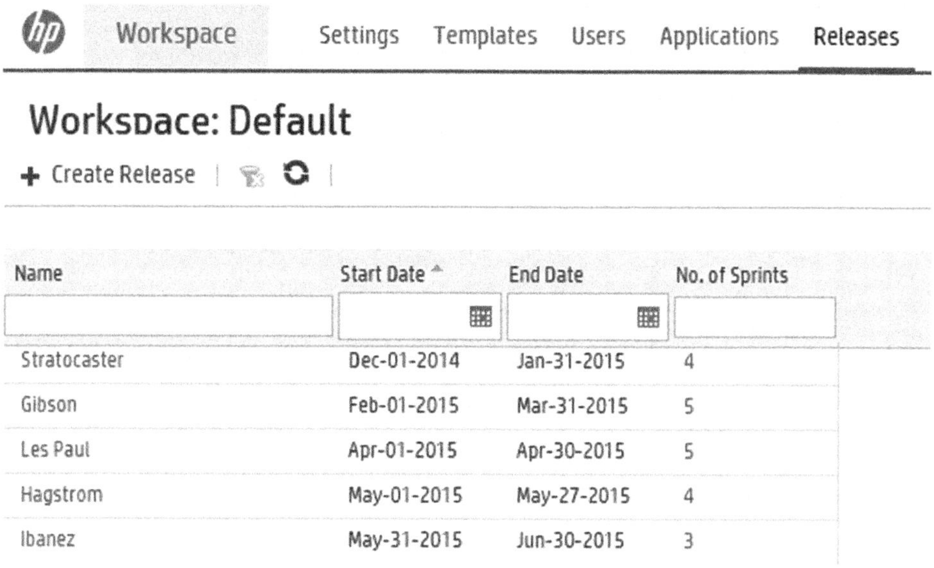

 Workspace   Settings   Templates   Users   Applications   **Releases**

Workspace: Default

+ Create Release

Name	Start Date ▲	End Date	No. of Sprints
Stratocaster	Dec-01-2014	Jan-31-2015	4
Gibson	Feb-01-2015	Mar-31-2015	5
Les Paul	Apr-01-2015	Apr-30-2015	5
Hagstrom	May-01-2015	May-27-2015	4
Ibanez	May-31-2015	Jun-30-2015	3

Figure 3-17. *Release setup*

The grid layout will show a list of releases, including their names, their timeline, and the number of sprints, and all columns are sortable.

Creating a New Release

From the grid toolbar, click Create Release, which will open the Create New Release page, as shown in Figure 3-18, where you will begin setting up a new release. Initially, you'll begin with the basic release details for your release by populating the Name and Description fields as you see fit. In the Release Time Frame section, set the Start Date and End Date fields according to your planned release time line, but be sure to make room for at least five sprints to follow up with the examples you build upon in this book. Specify the Sprint Duration value, which will automatically create initial sprints that are spread throughout the release, as specified by the Sprint Duration Units field.

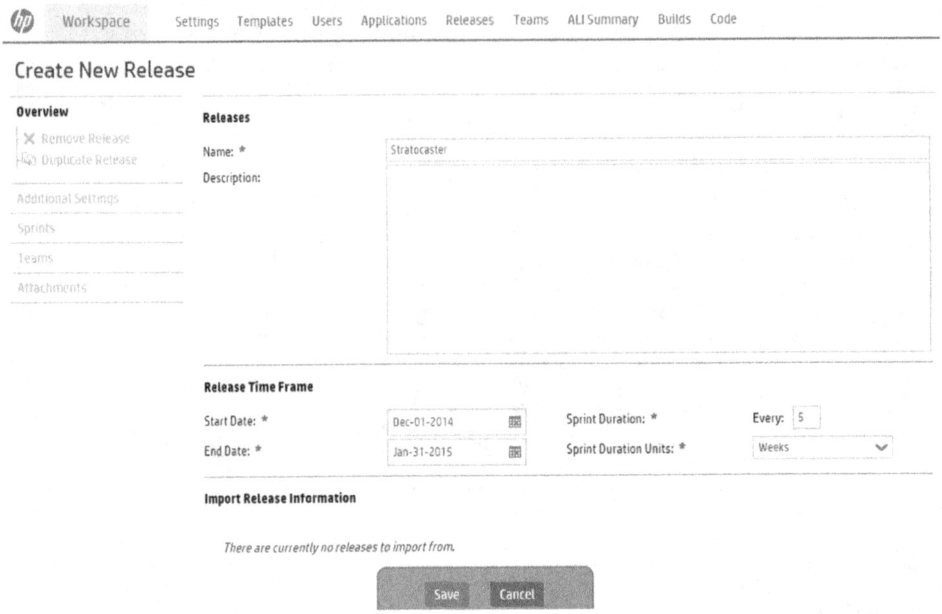

Figure 3-18. *Release setup*

If you have previously used Agile Manager and created a release, it is possible to import settings from a previous release using the Import Release Information option. Just select the check box and choose a source release to copy the settings from.

When you're done setting up the release details, click the Save button, and the release will be created, allowing you to continue to set up sprints and teams for this release. Figure 3-19 shows the Release Timeline section, which once created will feature a Gantt-like chart of the sprints in this release and highlight in green the current sprint and in blue the upcoming sprints. When the release is over and you are viewing it, the sprint color will be gray.

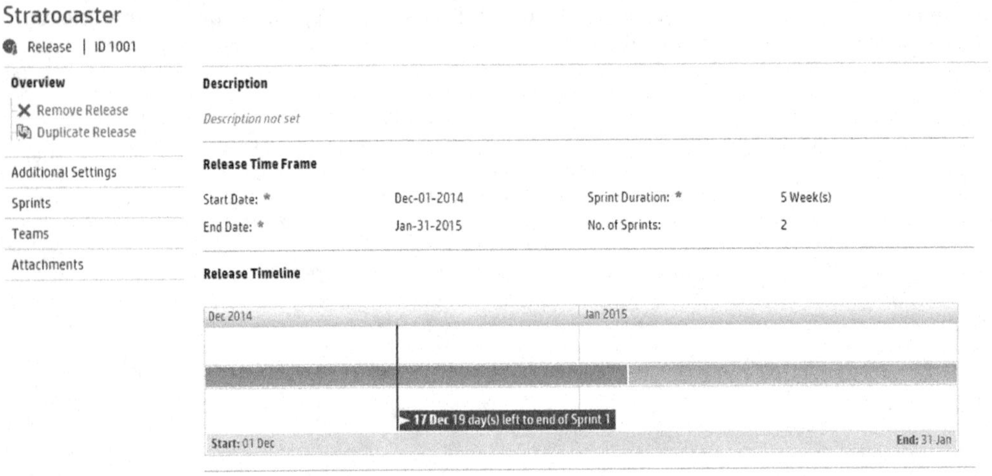

Figure 3-19. *Release timeline*

As mentioned, the release can also include attachments for documents and even links. To manage attachments, you'll navigate to the Attachments tab in the left panel of the release details area. The Attachments page will display the list of resources added to the release in the grid layout.

To add a resource, click the Add Attachment option in the grid toolbar, and the pop-up dialog shown in Figure 3-20 will appear.

Figure 3-20. *Release attachments creation*

The File option is toggled on by default for creating a document resource type from your own computer. In this case, simply click the Browse button to open the upload file dialog and choose the file. Fill in the Description field as necessary and click Add to save the attachment. Uploaded resources can't be edited, so to update a resource, you would need to either click the Delete option in the grid toolbar when the attachment is toggled on and re-upload it or add a new attachment and select the "Replace existing file" option.

You may sometimes be interested in making other team members aware of the resources added in the attachments list for a backlog item, or you simply may want to log this action. The resource file upload options allows you to select the "Add the description to comments" option, which will also create a comment on your behalf with the Description field set as the comment text. This is useful if you'd like to record the attachment action through the commenting system.

Adding online resources in the form of links to outside Agile Manager resources is made possible by selecting the URL option in the Add Attachment dialog and providing the URL and the name of the resource.

Managing Release Sprints

Even though you provided the number of sprints in this release and their duration and Agile Manager created the sprints layout for you automatically, you will still probably need to adjust the sprints.

To manage the release sprints, click the Sprints tab in the left panel. The Sprints page, as shown in Figure 3-21, will include sprint widgets, which show the sprint duration and number of sprints in a release, as well as the current sprint and the release dates.

Stratocaster

● Release | ID 1001

Overview	**Sprint Duration:**	5 Weeks		**Current Sprint(s):**	Sprint 1: Dec-01-2014 till Jan-04-2015
	No. of Sprints:	2 Sprint(s)		**Release Dates:**	Dec-01-2014 till Jan-31-2015
Additional Settings					

+ Add Sprint **+ Add Sprint to End of Release** ❖ Shift Sprints ✕ Remove from Release | 🗊 ◯ |

Name	Start Date ^	End Date	Assigned Teams
☐	[ ] 🔢	[ ] 🔢	
☐ Sprint 1 - (current)	Dec-01-2014	Jan-04-2015	No teams exist
☐ Sprint 2	Jan-05-2015	Jan-31-2015	No teams exist

(left panel tabs: Overview, Additional Settings, Sprints, Teams, Attachments)

Figure 3-21. *Sprint management*

The grid listing will display the sprints you created and allow for sorting and filtering by dates using the respective Start Date and End Date columns. The grid is itself is interactive and allows for inline editing of any field data by double-clicking it.

For sprints management, you can use the grid toolbar, which enables the following actions:

- *Add Sprint*: To add a sprint, you click this toolbar option and provide the sprint name, start date, end date, and assigned teams for this sprint. Teams can be assigned to different sprints, or all teams can be assigned on all sprints, which is the default when creating a new sprint.

- *Add Sprint to End of Release*: This is an added functionality, mainly for convenience, and will allow you to add a sprint to the end of the release, if no sprint was already created. It is usually good for adding late-release sprints such as feature freeze or code freeze.

- *Shift Sprint*: Shifting sprints is made possible by this toolbar option, and it allows you to move a sprint forward or backward by a specified day interval. Notice that shifting the sprints time won't adjust the rest of the sprints accordingly.

- *Remove from Release*: To delete a sprint, use this toolbar option.

For the sprints that were created in this release, go ahead rename the first sprint that was called Sprint 1 by Agile Manager to Bug Hunt and Planning instead. Next, adjust the release dates and make sure to add two sprints in the end of the release: Feature Freeze and Code Freeze.

Managing Release Teams

Agile Manager facilitates the sprints and backlog items assignment through the use of teams. Although it is possible to still work with no teams assigned or created, it wouldn't benefit you in the long run when you want to use the team buckets in the release backlog and widgets in the dashboard.

Whether you have just one team or you're working in multiple teams, such as component-based teams or feature-based teams, you're encouraged to create these teams per release. To begin managing your release teams, navigate to the Teams tab on the left panel, which will display the existing teams block widget representation. This page allows you to quickly view the team status and its member count, as shown in Figure 3-22.

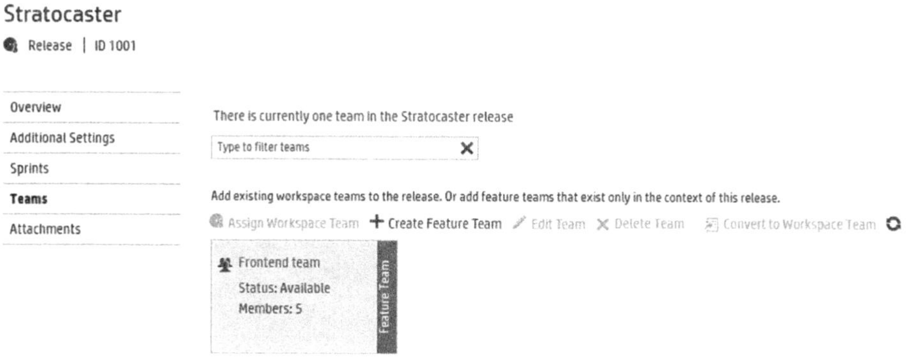

Figure 3-22. *Release teams*

The familiar grid toolbar allows you to easily access the team creation and editing actions. To begin, you'll create a new team by clicking the Create Feature Team option in the toolbar, which will open the Create New Team page. Name it the **Frontend team** and fill in the Name and Description fields. If this agile team is already experienced or you can estimate the velocity for it for a given sprint, then you can specify the story points in the Est. Sprint Velocity field. For this example, set this option to 20 story points per member per two-week sprint. When you're done, click the Save button.

Once the new team has been created, the page will show the first Overview tab at the left panel and will display the Availability & Velocity information. On this tab, you can configure the sprints in which this team will be available if required or just leave the default All Sprints option. As this team progresses to work on the sprints, the Overview tab will also display a widget showing a visual representation of the team's velocity in recent sprints. To delete a team, simply click the Remove Team option from the Overview tab panel.

Managing Team Members

To begin managing team members for this team, click the Team Members tab in the left panel of the team page, which will display the existing team members. To add a new member to this team, you click the Add Team Members option in the toolbar. The pop-up dialog shown in Figure 3-23 will appear; it allows you to select the users from the current workspace by simply selecting them from the list. If this is a large list, you can sort it by using the Full Name or Login Name column and also filter by them. Choose some team members and click the Add to Team button to close the dialog.

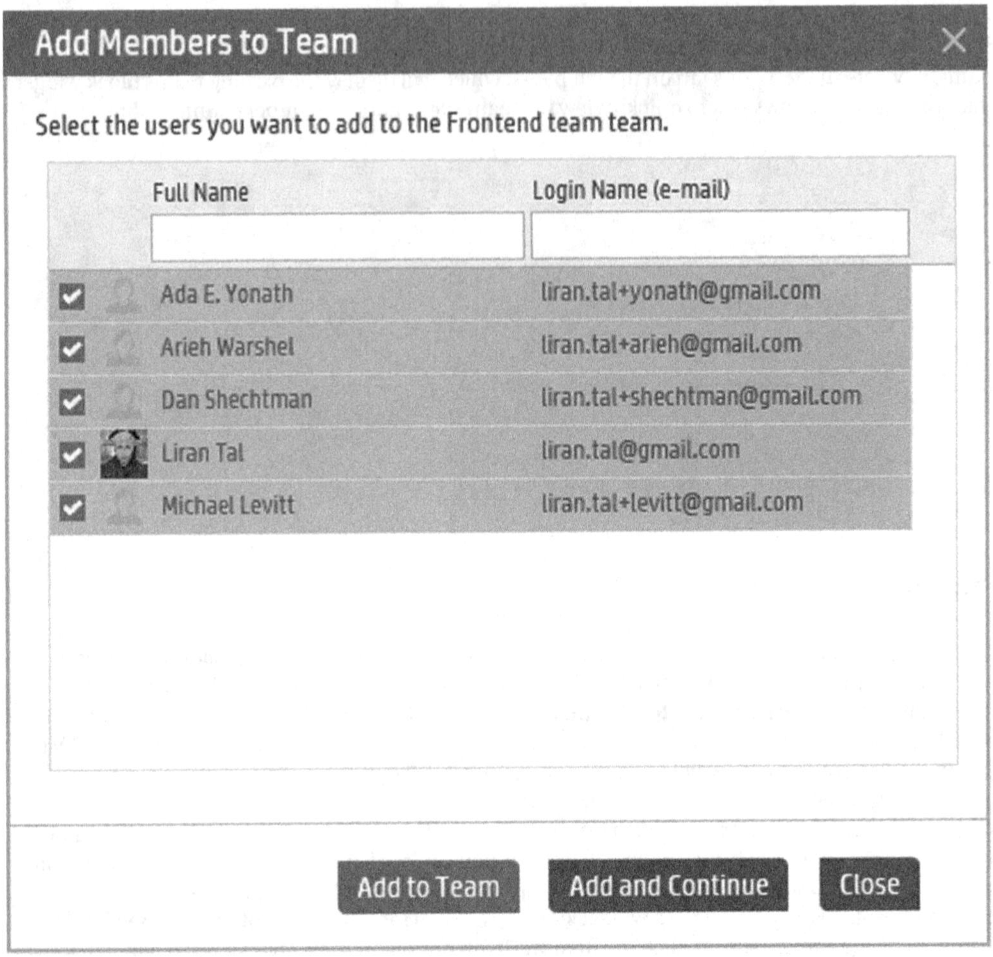

Figure 3-23. *Agile Manager Release team member added*

Once added, the member's listing will show up in a thumbnail box–style view with a vertical scroll bar so you can browse through the users in this team. To gain further insight into any team member, simply click its thumbnail box, and the right-side area will show the user's personal contact information (see Figure 3-24).

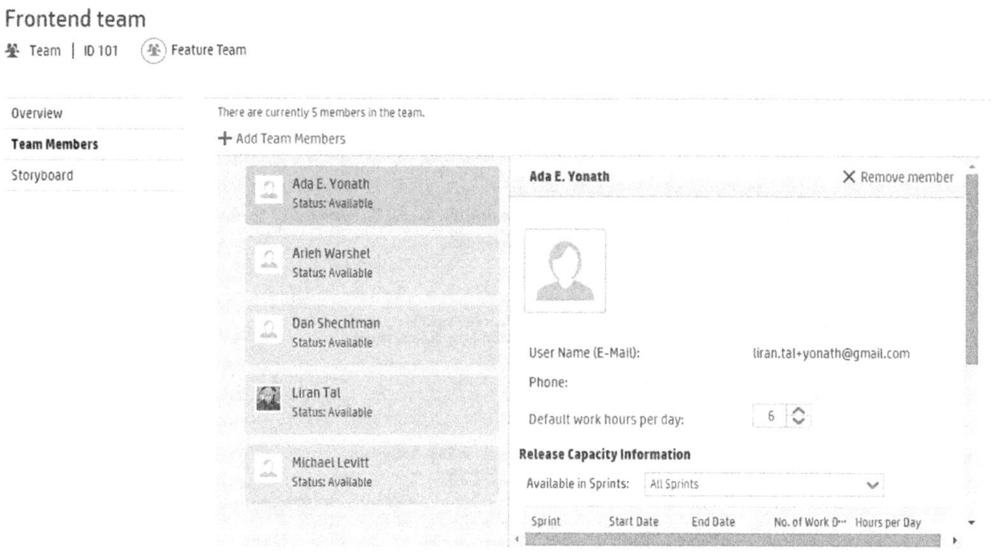

Frontend team

♟ Team | ID 101 (♟) Feature Team

Figure 3-24. *Release team member management*

The team member view also allows the user to fine-tune his individual settings for the release, as shown in Figure 3-24:

- *Default work hours per day*: Set the amount of time in hours for which this user will be available for the current team.

- *Available in Sprints*: Set the sprints for this team that this member will be available for.

■ **Note**   Since team members may participate in more than one team, they can individually be further configured to be available for a specified amount of time or in different sprints, as necessary. The Release Capacity Information setting allows this fine-tuning if necessary using the previously mentioned settings.

To remove a team member, click their thumbnail box to expand their information view and then click the "Remove member" option from the title bar at the right.

Release Configuration

You can customize a release to meet different team characteristics and thus provide a flexible configuration for managers to set up.

To begin customizing your release setup, navigate to Workspace ➤ Releases and the release you just created. Then on the release page, click the Additional Settings tab in the left panel (see Figure 3-25).

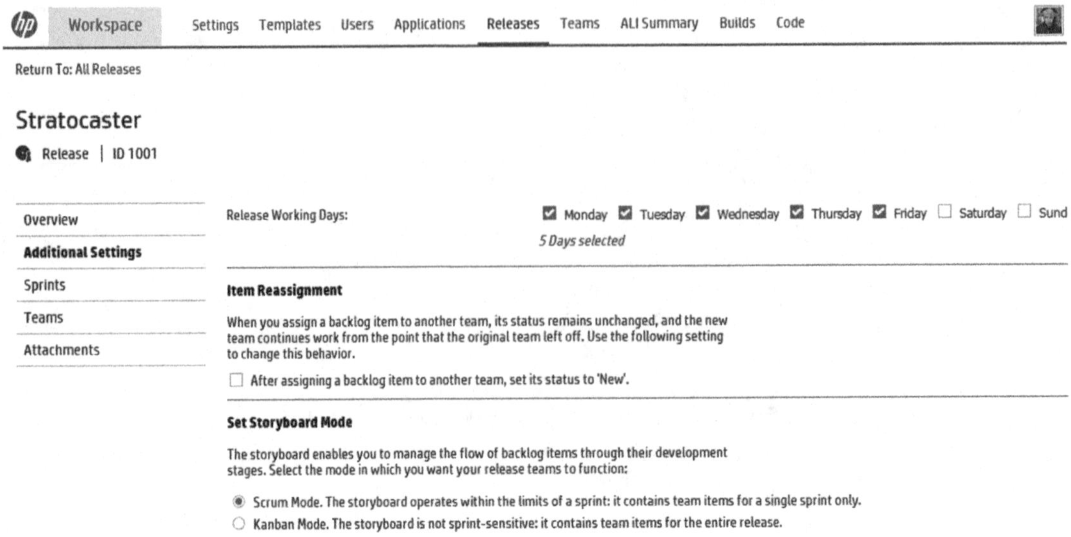

Figure 3-25. *Release settings*

Let's review the options available for customizing the release as shown in Figure 3-25:

- *Release Working Days*: Whether you're managing a release that spans multinational team members or your team is working on a five-day week schedule that begins on Monday, it's easy to adjust the working days accordingly. Working days affect the release setup, sprints planning, and dashboards with the weekly availability of teams, or individual members.

- *Item Reassignment*: When items from the backlog get re-assigned from one team to another or from one team member to another, the status of the backlog item stays the same. If you want the status of a backlog item to be set to New each time it is re-assigned, select this setting.

- *Set Storyboard Mode*: The storyboard workflow can be set to run in a release-oriented fashion, meaning that it will reflect backlog items for the entire release, or rather, it can be run in cycles of sprints. This setting will configure the behavior.

You'll select the Item Reassignment setting because this will make sure that no items stay in a limbo state when they are transferred from one team member to another and will ensure that they get reevaluated because of a New status when they are dealt with in the future. The rest of the settings can keep their defaults, but you can change them as you see fit for your setup.

Summary

In this chapter, you learned about configuring Agile Manager site settings; setting up workspaces, users, and the example software project's applications; and tweaking the default settings. You also learned how to prepare a release, set up the sprints for it, and build and manage your teams.

CHAPTER 4

■ ■ ■

Building the Product Backlog

In the previous chapter, you learned how to set up and configure Agile Manager's site settings, how to manage users, and how to create workspaces. You reviewed how to assign users to workspaces, customize the workspace settings, and add your applications. You also learned how a release is created and managed through Agile Manager's configuration mode and explored how to manage release sprints and set up teams.

In this chapter, you'll learn how to work with Agile Manager to build your product backlog. We'll cover the following topics:

- Managing themes

- Managing features and streamlining feature-oriented releases

- Viewing and managing product backlog items, as well as some unique actions for Agile Manager such as breaking up a user story into multiple items and converting them to features

The Product Backlog

The product backlog contains a list of items that generally describe the requirements of the product or bugs that need to be addressed. High-level backlog items such as themes and features consist of an organized set of requirements, whereas more detailed low-level items such as user stories and defects consist of the actual product backlog items that require addressing, thus completing the themes and features.

To begin working on the product backlog and continue managing your release and team life cycle, let's switch back from the configuration area by clicking the gray gear icon (which is where we left off in the previous chapter); then navigate to Product Backlog view using the main navigation bar.

The Product Backlog view allows you to manage the high-level requirements through the Themes and Features sections; it also allows you to manage the product's backlog item list of user stories and defects through the Backlog section, as shown in Figure 4-1.

Figure 4-1. *Product Backlog view*

The Product Backlog view features the Application contextual filter, which allows you to easily switch between the various product applications you've created. The grid layout allows you to manage all the backlog items and has left and right panels.

- *Filter by and Group by*: In the left panel, this enables quick access to filtering the grid items and grouping them by specific fields.

- *Planning: Releases bucket*: In the right panel, the releases bucket enables you to quickly view the status of a release from a top-level perspective of backlog items and features.

All user story and defect backlog items need to be associated with a feature and a theme, so you will begin with managing themes and features and then move on to managing your product backlog.

Themes

A theme is a high-level function that can be thought of as a description of a functional area within your product. Some examples for themes for web applications re notifications, which describes your e-mail, and the messaging notification system.

Adding a Theme

To begin working with themes, navigate to Product Backlog ➤ Themes to add your first theme. You'll build on the theme example and add a theme called Notifications. From the grid toolbar, click Add Item and set Type to Theme, set Name to Notifications, add an attachment if you'd like, and set Application to Backend and Frontend using the drop-down options.

Once added, the new theme will appear in the list. By right-clicking the item from the grid, you can access it by clicking View Details. In the theme's view, as shown in Figure 4-2, you can further adjust the settings for the theme, such as adding a description, adding comments, and attaching resources. The theme also includes a progress indication that aggregates the number of stories and defects, as well as the story points set for these backlog items.

Figure 4-2. *Theme view*

Features can also be managed through the theme view page by clicking the Features tab in the left panel and managing them per theme.

Managing Themes

In the Product Backlog ➤ Themes area, you can manage all of your product's themes, as shown in Figure 4-3. The default display grid listing has some useful columns, such as the following:

- *Rank*: Enables you to prioritize themes by ranking them.

- *Features*: Shows the number of features created for each theme. This is a good way to find out where you need to focus the most attention as time progresses with developing your product.

- *Progress*: Shows a progress bar that indicates the current state of completed story points versus the total planned story points for all backlog items. Hovering over the progress bar will also reveal information about the number of user stories and defects associated with this theme.

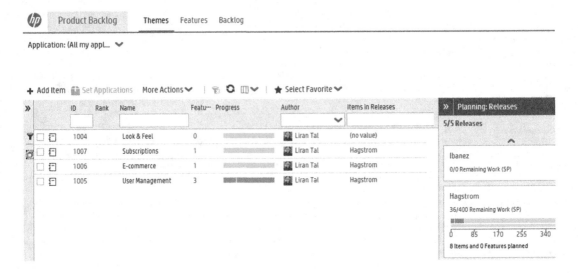

Figure 4-3. *Theme backlog*

Common theme actions can be found in the grid toolbar, and some of the more relevant items include the following:

- *Set Applications*: If a theme should be associated with more applications, it can be easily selected, and then clicking this option will allow you to update the applications this theme is associated with. You should note that themes will automatically be associated with applications that are set for the theme's features, user stories, or defects, and they cannot be removed from the theme level.

- *Export Backlog to Excel*: Exporting data from Agile Manager may be required if you need to create some executive reports. Exporting a theme backlog to Excel or CSV is easy through the More Actions drop-down toolbar option.

Features

After defining your product's themes, you can move on to managing features. When adding features, you will create a descriptive functional requirement, business requirement, or architectural requirement to be developed. Features are associated with themes and form a hierarchy tree between themes and the lower-level user stories or defects.

To review and manage features, let's navigate to Product Backlog ➤ Features; you'll see a grid layout view similar to Figure 4-4.

Figure 4-4. *Features view*

Adding Features

To begin filling up your product backlog with features, let's create a new feature by clicking the Add Item in the grid toolbar. In the pop-up dialog for adding a new feature, the Type field should already be set to Feature. To continue with the Notifications theme, let's set the feature's Name field to "Support incoming forum posts through e-mail." Set the Theme field accordingly. Furthermore, it is possible to provide a resource such as a function specification document with the Attachments field, set the Application field accordingly, and even provide an initial Feature Story Points estimation. Click the Save and Add Another button to apply this feature and go ahead and create some more features to fill in the feature backlog. The following are some ideas for features:

- "Allow users to subscribe to e-mail notifications"
- "Support HTML in e-mail notifications"
- "Support file attachments in e-mail notifications"
- "Provide a UI to manage user's subscriptions"

To further set up features properly, you will need to edit the feature by clicking its ID in the grid listing, which opens the single feature edit page, as shown in Figure 4-5.

Return To: Features

Allow users to upload picture

📄 Feature | ID 1010

Overview	Description				Related People	
✉ Send by E-Mail	Allowing users to upload pictures using the Set User Profile area				Owner:	👤 Liran Tal
Backlog Items					Author:	👤 Liran Tal
Attachments	**Details**				**Attachments**	
History	Priority:	1-High	Modified:	Dec-18-2014 21:33:12	*Drop Here*	📎
Development Activity	Theme:	User Management	Applications:	Backend; Frontend; Messaging and Notifications	No attachments	

Priority: 1-High Modified: Dec-18-2014 21:33:12
Theme: User Management Applications: Backend; Frontend; Messaging and Notifications

Planned vs. Actual (Story points)
Total stories: 1
Total defects: 1

Creation Date:	Dec-18-2014	Creation Time:	04:51:52
Feature Type:	Business	Initial Estimate:	M

Show More...

0 6 12 18 24 30

☐ **Release Plan**

Release:	*No value*	Feature Story Points:	30

⊞ **Comments (0)** 💬 Add Comment

Figure 4-5. *Features edit page*

The feature Overview tab on the left side will be selected and displayed by default and will provide access to the following important fields that need to be set for the feature:

- *Description*: Adding a description to features is an important task and allows you to describe the feature further than just its title.

- *Related People*: The right sidebar displays a few detail blocks, and this one allows you to set the owner of the feature. It's common that a single person will be responsible for owning a feature end-to-end. For this purpose, you can set the Owner field for a feature to any member of this workspace.

- *Priority*: Features, just like user stories, share the priority field and enable you to set a straightforward priority for a feature: High, Medium, and Low.

- *Feature Type*: If a feature serves the purpose of providing an architectural basis or development that is required to support the product, or other features, then the type can be set to Architectural. On the other hand, if the feature is about meeting a functional requirement, its type can be set to Business. This setting allows for easily differentiating the functional deliverable features from R&D tasks such as server maintenance, automation and testing tasks, and so on.

- *Initial Estimate*: A quick measuring scale for estimating the size of feature is the so-called shirt sizes estimation, which allows a range of values including XS for extra-small, M for medium, and XL for extra-large. While this isn't an accurate estimate, it enables you to quickly estimate features and plan features for release.

- *Release*: This setting allows you to set a feature for a specific release. By clicking it, the Feature Planning pop-up dialog will display and enable you to quickly set associated backlog items with this feature to the specified release. Learn more in the "Feature Planning" section.

Let's go through the features you've created and set these settings for each feature so you can use these fields later in the grid layout to filter and sort the features backlog.

Another important field that features have is the Status setting, through which Agile Manager provides a way to track the feature's life-cycle progress. The Status field offers a granular detailed level of the current state of the feature. Let's review each of the options and the recommended definitions you will be using them for.

- *New*: When features are just added to the backlog, they are set to this initial default option.

- *Defined*: When a feature's description is provided and has considerable more information than just the title, when its priority has been set, and when its initial estimate has also been set, the feature is set to Defined.

- *Scoped*: When the feature is estimated with story points and has backlog items created for it already (user stories), it is set to Scoped.

- *Accepted*: When the feature has been reviewed by the product owner and the feature team for the feature implementation information, it is set to Accepted.

The rest of the states, In Progress and Done, are obvious. The Descoped status can be set for features that were planned for a release but didn't get into it or for the feature that were abandoned.

The Backlog Items tab in the left sidebar allows you to easily access any user stories or defects that are associated with this feature. From this tab, it is possible to quickly add a user story or defect for the current feature or simply browse through the list of existing backlog items. The listing includes the number of story points set for each item, its status, the assigned user, and also a progress bar indication for tasks estimation.

Ordering the Features Grid

The default grid layout can be cumbersome, and the item listing can grow quite easily because it doesn't use any filters, which may become a hassle when you want to manage your features. Because you may be visiting the Features backlog view often to track progress for features and generally manage them, such as adding documentation or setting estimation accordingly, in this section you will organize the grid layout differently to allow for quick and easy access to your features.

To begin organizing the features grid, let's first navigate back to Product Backlog ➤ Features and choose your columns by clicking the table icon with the down arrow from the grid toolbar and toggling on the column options you're interested in. The following are usually important columns: ID, Rank, Name, Agg. Story Points, User Stories, Defects, Priority, Progress, Owner, Status, Theme, and Applications.

░ **Note**   When adding a new column, it will always be added at the end, to the right of the table grid. If at any point in time you want to clear any sorting, filtering, or ordering of columns, you can click the table icon for column selection and choose the first option at the top called "Restore default display."

The recommended columns order is as specified in the columns list, but you may order the columns as you want by simply dragging the column from its header text and moving it left or right to change its position in the grid layout.

Filtering the Features Grid

The grid listing can be tweaked for certain column filters and values through the left panel. In the left side of the grid, locate the filter icon, or simply click the right arrow in the top-left panel of the grid. This will slide open the Filter sidebar, which allows you to also define any group via settings.

Click the Filter by tab in the left Filter sidebar, and then you can add filters by clicking the Add Property option and selecting the Release filter. Once added, select the release you've just added from the drop-down options.

■ **Note** When adding filters to the grid view, the toolbar indicates that filters exist by highlighting the filter icon on the toolbar in blue. This icon shows up with an *x* on top of it, which resets the filter. It may happen quite often that you will work with filters and not realize why you may be missing some items from the list. If in doubt, use the toolbar filter icon to reset any filters, grouping, or sorting.

Sorting the Features Grid

You can further organize the features backlog view by sorting the features based on their Priority column. You can get quick access to sorting columns by clicking the column header with the column title, which will toggle the sorting to ascending or descending order.

Another way to access a column's settings is to hover over the column header; a gray down arrow appears to the right of the text. Clicking it will reveal a context menu with the following options:

- *Sort Ascending*: Sorts the items list based on this column in ascending order

- *Sort Descending*: Sorts the items list based on this column in descending order

- *Group by*: Turns the features backlog items into a grouped item listing, which creates a hierarchy view inside the grid layout of collapsed or expanded items

If you've chosen either to sort the features backlog by ascending order based on the Priority column or to group the results by this column, the result should look like Figure 4-6.

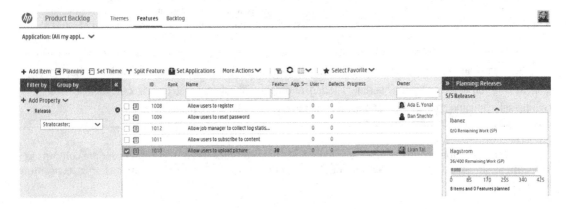

Figure 4-6. *Features view*

Ranking Features

When you added features before, you saw how to set their priority, and now you have learned how to sort or group the features list by their priority, but priorities might not always be enough. Imagine having five features, all of which are high-priority items, assigned to the team developer or the same feature team. Out of the five, which should be picked up first? It may not be trivial or even possible to begin working on more than one feature at a time. While the priority field makes sense from a functional architect and business perspective to differentiate the importance of features, there's a need to further fine-tune the order of importance for features.

Feature ranking comes into the picture to provide real items with prioritization by explicitly setting a rank value for each feature, thus forcing a differentiated set of backlog items. This ranking can then be used to better prioritize the release backlog or the sprint backlog for important features or user stories to take on.

While the ranking seems not present at first glance when viewing the grid listing for the features view, in practice every time you create a feature, it is given a default rank, beginning at 1 for the highest-ranking feature (or the first one that was created out of the feature list).

■ **Note**   Ranking doesn't work on grouped items, so if you choose to group the features backlog by the Priority column, you should undo it or completely reset the filters using the filter icon in the grid toolbar to completely reset the feature backlog view and return it to its original state.

To begin ranking the feature backlog, make sure you're not in grouped view and then click the Rank column to sort by rank. Doing so will sort the feature backlog in ascending order from the highest-ranking feature with a value of 1 to the lowest feature, which was probably created last. To change the ranking for features, simply drag one or more features by toggling them and move them up or down in the grid listing, as shown in Figure 4-7.

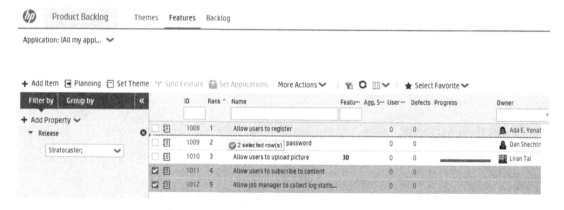

Figure 4-7. *Ranking features*

Another way to rank backlog items is to simply double-click the rank field on a feature and on the inline editing to set its numeric value to any other value. The rest of the features will shift their values up or down, depending on their ranking position in the list.

■ **Note** If you are going to change filters to show more or less features in the listing, you will notice that backlog items do not retain a fixed numeric value for their ranking position field. They are rather ranked relative to other features in the currently displayed listing.

Managing the Features Backlog

To begin working on features, you'll review how features are planned and several characteristics of the feature backlog that enable easy and proper management of features.

Feature Planning

Quick access to feature planning allows you to easily update the feature status, as well as update all associated backlog items to it from one place. To understand how this works, let's toggle on one or more features from the features backlog and then click the Planning option in the grid toolbar and review the available options, as shown in Figure 4-8.

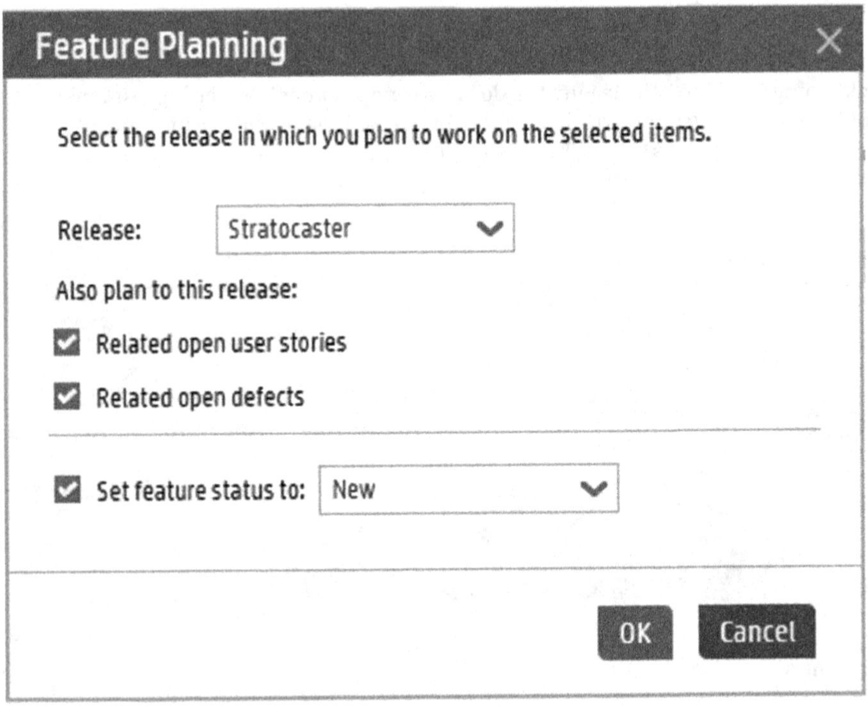

Figure 4-8. *Feature planning*

- *Release*: If this feature isn't assigned to any release, it can be easily assigned by choosing the desired release, or if it is already assigned, then the release can be adjusted for this feature through the drop-down options.

- *Plan open user stories for this release*: By toggling on the Related open user stories option, any backlog items that are associated with this feature will be assigned to the release chosen.

- *Plan open defects for this release*: This is similar to user stories; selecting the "Plan open defects" option will also assign any of the open defects to the chosen release.

- *Feature status*: The "Set feature status" option allows you to easily update a very granular status setting for a feature, at any point in time.

The Feature Planning Bucket

Another way to assign a feature to a release and also view a whole lot of information in a dashboard view is through the Planning: Releases bucket, as shown in Figure 4-9.

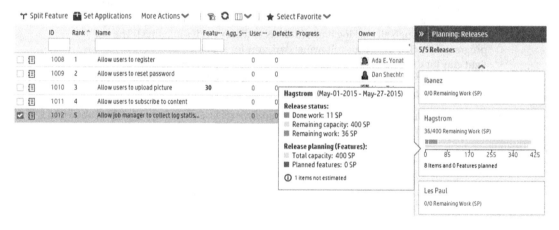

Figure 4-9. *Feature planning bucket*

To begin working with it, navigate to the Product Backlog ➤ Features page and expand the right sidebar by clicking the arrows pointing to the left to open it. At this point, you can either view the entire features backlog by having no filters on the grid view or simply filter based on the desired features you want to add to the current release.

The Planning: Releases bucket lists all releases by default, so you'll begin by selecting only the current release for which you want to plan the features for. To do this, click the 1/1 Releases link that appears at the top of the bucket column. This link will list more releases as you add them and will show them in the format of 10/10, and so on, according to your filters. Once you click the releases link, an in-place options window will display to allow you to select the releases you want to list in the bucket. If there is more than just one release, then select the release you created in the previous chapter to work with.

To add a feature, with all of its associated backlog items, simply drag the feature from the grid listing and into the bucket area. The release bucket will now contain more details, and if you hover over it, a pop-up will display to the left of it with more detailed information.

Let's now review the information available through the release bucket.

- The release name and time frame will show up at the top part of the release bucket entry, with the release name being clickable. This allows you to quickly navigate to the release backlog to view and manage backlog items such as user stories and defects.

- Release capacity information will show up at the bottom part of the release bucket entry and will feature total and remaining work by counting the story points aggregated through all backlog items (defects and user stories together). The progress bar will indicate the following: dark gray for features planned to the release, light gray for the available or remaining release capacity in story points, red for story points that exceed the available capacity, green for completed story points, and lastly blue for open backlog items with story points remaining.

Agile Manager offers much broader information to analyze release planning properly as shown in Figure 4-10, which you can take a glance at by clicking the Remaining Work (SP) link in the bucket's capacity information area.

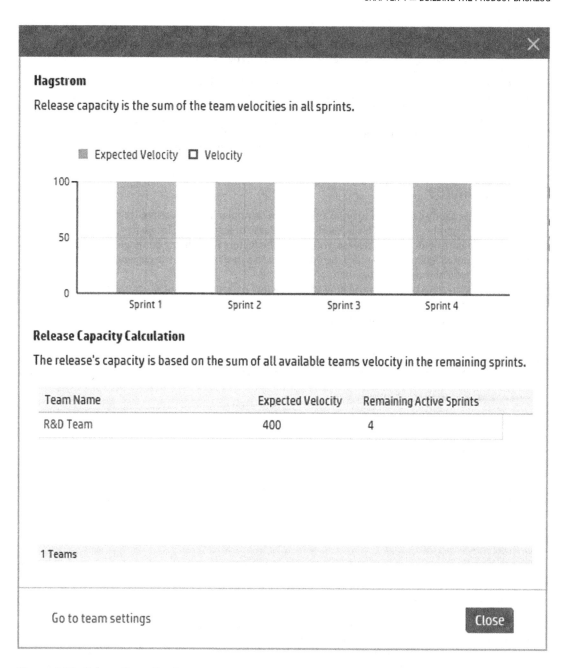

Figure 4-10. Release Capacity view

- The Release Capacity view will then open up in a pop-up window, as shown in Figure 4-10, and will provide information on the overall release velocity of the team through the Expected Velocity and actual Velocity columns.

- The velocity in each sprint can be seen through the visual bar chart widget.

- Team capacity information is also listed in the table to show the expected capacity for each team, as was configured for the team, as well as the remaining active sprints. Clicking the relevant team or using the "Go to team settings" link will navigate to the Configuration console to further configure team velocity information.

Splitting Features

Feature splitting is handy if you need to break up the currently open items associated with a certain feature and move them to another feature. This is handy if the release or feature time frame has ended and you need to wrap up the feature of the current release, without all the feature items being completed. In this case, splitting the feature will allow you to move the open items to a new feature in the current release or for a new feature planned for a new release altogether.

To split a feature, let's begin by navigating to the Product Backlog ➤ Features page and click the feature you're interested in splitting out. Once it's selected, the Split Feature option on the grid toolbar will be enabled for you to click and will display a pop-up, as shown in Figure 4-11.

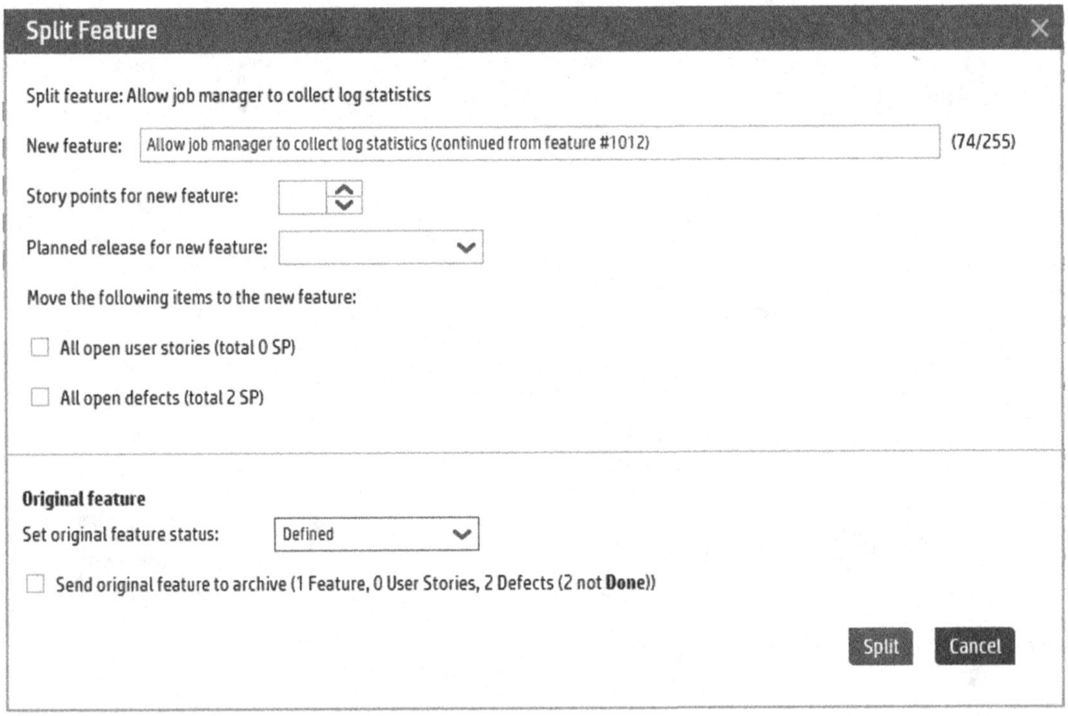

Split Feature ✕

Split feature: Allow job manager to collect log statistics

New feature: `Allow job manager to collect log statistics (continued from feature #1012)` (74/255)

Story points for new feature: [   ]

Planned release for new feature: [▼]

Move the following items to the new feature:

☐ All open user stories (total 0 SP)

☐ All open defects (total 2 SP)

Original feature

Set original feature status: [Defined   ▼]

☐ Send original feature to archive (1 Feature, 0 User Stories, 2 Defects (2 not **Done**))

[Split] [Cancel]

Figure 4-11. Splitting a feature

The New feature field will already be set with a default name that is made up of the current feature name with additional origin information for the feature you're splitting now. The "Story points for new feature" field allows you to quickly set this information; however, it's not required, and probably this will still be unknown when splitting the feature. Whether the split feature will be available in the current release or in a new release, you can use the setting "Planned release."

It is most likely that when the need comes to split feature, work has already begun on it, which means you will probably have open backlog items (defects or user stories). By using the setting " Move the following fields to the new feature," you can select these backlog items, and any open items will be associated only with the new feature you're creating. Agile Manager will also point out the total story points set for any of these backlog items.

Additionally, it is possible to use the "Set original feature status" setting, which defaults to a "Defined status" option.

Backlog Items

On the Product Backlog ➤ Backlog page, you can find all the backlog items of type user stories or defects that were ever created. You can access this page to find a user story or defect of interest that you'd like to locate and track its history. Another reason for visiting this page is if you're migrating from another system to Agile Manager and need to migrate your data; then by using the More Actions option on the grid toolbar, it is possible to select the Import Backlog option and provide an Excel or CSV-formatted file to import any user stories or defects straight into the product backlog.

Adding user stories or defects through the Backlog page isn't common or recommended since this is the Product Backlog area and there is probably no reason to add a general user story to the overall product backlog unless it is added by the product owner or it is already known in advance that the user story isn't going to be handled in any current or planned future release. Defects that are found and are preknown to not be part of any release but just need to be recorded in the product's backlog for tracking reasons can also be added on the Backlog page; however, you will still see how it is possible to add both defects as well as user stories for the product backlog, or any other release, through the Release Backlog area.

■ **Note** The R&D team will concentrate their work with Agile Manager in the context of a release backlog and release Sprint pages, and thus any backlog items will be created in the relevant release and sprint.

You'll add a user story to the backlog to be able to explore some of the actions provided only in the backlog page. To begin, click the Add Item option in the grid toolbar and fill in a name for the user story such as **As a user, I want to post forum topics by sending an e-mail.** You can also populate the remaining fields in the form, but it isn't mandatory at the moment, and the Type and Name fields are the only required fields. Don't worry, we will revisit adding user stories and defects in the next chapter.

Breaking User Stories

Breaking user stories is quite useful when stories are being created in the beginning and later when they are estimated, throughout a planning poker session, for example, and the user story results in a large story points estimation that requires breaking up the original user story.

To begin, let's make sure that in the Product Backlog ➤ Backlog page, the Backlog Items View option is selected. Select a user story from the items in the grid to make sure it is selected; then click More Actions in the grid toolbar and choose the Break Story option.

When a story is broken up, the original story becomes a group story with all the newly created user stories associated with it (much like with features and items associated with them). New stories that are broken apart from the original user story inherit the original user story's acceptance tests and tasks. Any attachments that were added to the original user story will remain available, in the form of the new group story.

■ **Note** The group story's original estimation for story points is removed, and a group story's story points are the aggregated sum of all of its child stories.

Figure 4-12 shows how to create the new stories from the original by simply filling in the New Story Name field, which will default to the original story's name with a postfix of the text "part 1," and by filling in the Story Points field if this information is available at the time of creating the broken-apart stories. To create the story, click the Add button to the center right of the pop-up; you're welcome to create any additional child user stories as required. When you're finished, click the Break button.

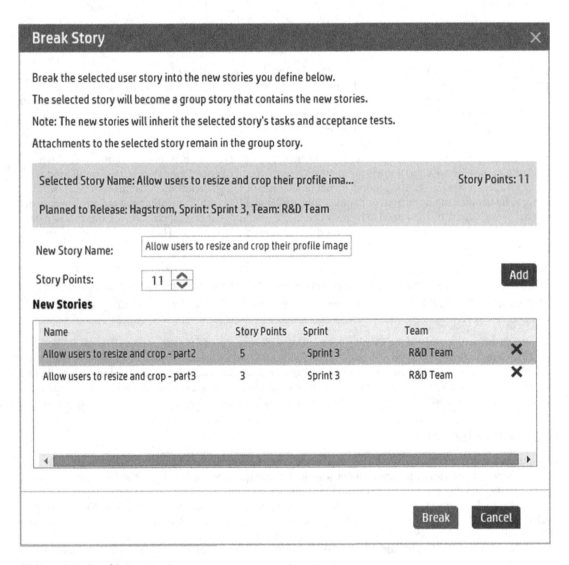

Figure 4-12. Breaking a user story

Once you're done breaking up a story into multiple child user stories, the items in the Backlog page will refresh, and you will see the newly added user stories.

■ **Note**   You will notice that the child stories look just like any other user story, and there's really no other way to tell that they belong to a group story. At this point, you will also notice that the original user story is no longer listed in the backlog items list; this is because it has been converted to a group story. It is not deleted or thrown away; it will simply be available in the group stories view.

To work with group stories, you'll need to click the Group Stories View option above the grid toolbar, which will reveal all of your created group stories. As shown in Figure 4-13, this view will list group stories as well as regular user stories by default. It is still easy to tell in this view if an item is a group story by its icon, which shows up in the Type column, as can be seen for the group story just created. To filter out the regular stories and show just group stories, click the Type column, and select the Group Story option only.

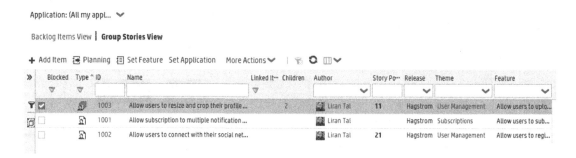

Figure 4-13.   *Group stories view*

From the group stories view, an additional column, Children, is added and will specify how many child stories are created for this item. If the column is clicked, it will change the grid listing to display the child stories but will also keep the original filter for the group stories view. Another way to view the child stories and also manage a group story is by clicking its ID column in the grid listing to edit it. Click to edit the group story you just created.

In the group story edit mode, you can already notice the less detailed information, and to manage the child user stories, simply click the Child Stories tab in the left sidebar.

Converting User Stories to Features

Converting user stories into features comes in handy when the product owner or the R&D team lead adds user stories at the product backlog level. This can often happen when a requirement starts out as something small that may seem to the product owner like a user story that can be implemented in a sprint but ends up being a much larger work.

Another case for converting user stories into features may take place when the team realizes that a user story is actually part of another feature, often as part of a bigger set of work that needs to be done, and at that point, it's easy enough to simply convert it into a feature and even keep the original user story that records the work (acceptance tests, tasks, and such that were already added to it).

Converting a user story is another option you can find in the More Actions option on the grid toolbar, on the Product Backlog ➤ Backlog page. Select a user story in the grid listing and choose the Convert to Feature option, which will open a pop-up, as shown in Figure 4-14.

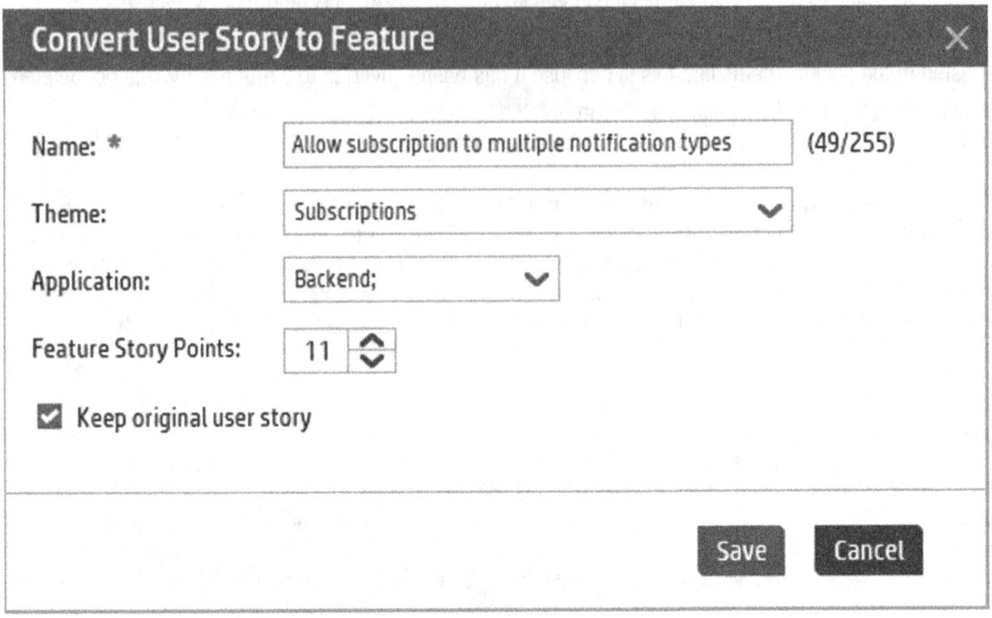

Figure 4-14. *Converting a user story to a feature*

The Name field will default to the user story field, and since you are converting to a feature, you should also set the Theme and Application fields accordingly. As mentioned, it is possible to also retain the user story as is and automatically associate it with the feature you're creating by toggling on the "Keep original user story" option, which is set by default. Otherwise, toggle it off, and the user story will be removed in favor of the new feature.

Summary

In this chapter, you learned how to manage themes and features. You reviewed the themes grid and the features grid and how to manage features, watch their progress through the release planning bucket, rank features, plan them, and split them up when needed. You also reviewed the product backlog items and learned about managing user stories in groups, as well as how to convert them to features.

CHAPTER 5

■ ■ ■

Streamlining Work in the Release Backlog

In the previous chapter, you learned how to prepare the product backlog from the themes and features perspective. You also reviewed briefly how to create user stories, but this was merely for the purpose of learning to create group stories and convert stories to features.

In this chapter, you'll learn how to use Agile Manager to prepare your release and streamline common research and development (R&D) tasks. More specifically, we will cover the following topics:

- Working in the sprint backlog and the release backlog

- Managing user stories

- Managing defects

- Facilitating a release retrospective process

Working in the Release Backlog

Unlike the product backlog, which consists of items for the entire product, the release backlog contains items only for the release you're viewing. More specifically, features that you created in the previous chapter and assigned to a release are not manageable through the release backlog. Work in the release backlog is meant to enable the management and streamlining of work related to user stories and defects.

To begin working in the release backlog, navigate to the Release Management area (see Figure 5-1) and confirm that the Release Backlog page is set for display.

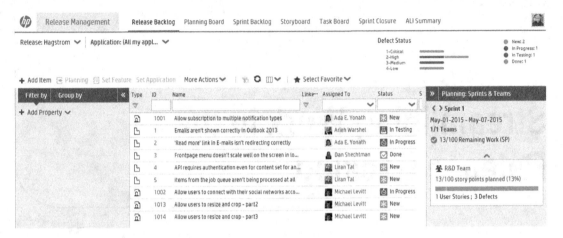

Figure 5-1. *The Release Backlog page*

The Release Management area, as shown in Figure 5-1, provides access to the following pages:

- *Release Backlog*: This page allows you to view and manage all release backlog items, including sprints and teams, through widgets.

- *Planning Board*: This page allows you to view and manage the release from a broader perspective by visualizing the release contents in the form of tiles; the tiles are spread across a customized set of columns and rows.

- *Sprint Backlog*: This page allows you to view and manage a specific sprint's backlog items. This page is similar to the release backlog and can be thought of as an instance of it for a specific sprint.

- *Storyboard*: This page allows you to view and manage the release in Kanban mode.

- *Task Board*: This page resembles the agile methodology's sticky notes for visualizing a release content through each sprint's tasks.

- *Sprint Closure*: This page allows you to record and formalize a sprint's retrospective, as well as view the sprint's status and summary.

- *ALI Summary*: This page allows you to view the release status from the perspectives of builds, code commits, code reviews, and more.

It is also important to notice that the Release Backlog page features the Release contextual filter and the Application contextual filter, which allow you to easily toggle through different applications and releases.

In this chapter, you will focus on the Release Backlog and sprint-related pages, namely, Sprint Backlog and Sprint Closure.

Working with User Stories

User stories are essential backlog items and have quite a few capabilities in Agile Manager; for example, you can easily streamline a flexible R&D workflow to accommodate more than a few agile practices.

■ **Note**   User stories, as well as any other views generated by Agile Manager, can be identified in the grid listing by their icon. It looks like a user with a piece of paper in the background.

Even though it is possible to add user stories from the Release Backlog page to begin your work with user stories, let's navigate to the Release Management ➤ Sprint Backlog page. You will learn how to work in the sprint backlog in the next section, but for now you'll focus on adding and managing a user story.

Adding a User Story

Whether you're at the Sprint Backlog page or the Release Backlog page, the grid toolbar will show the Add Item option. Clicking it opens a pop-up dialog that will default to a user story backlog item, as shown in Figure 5-2.

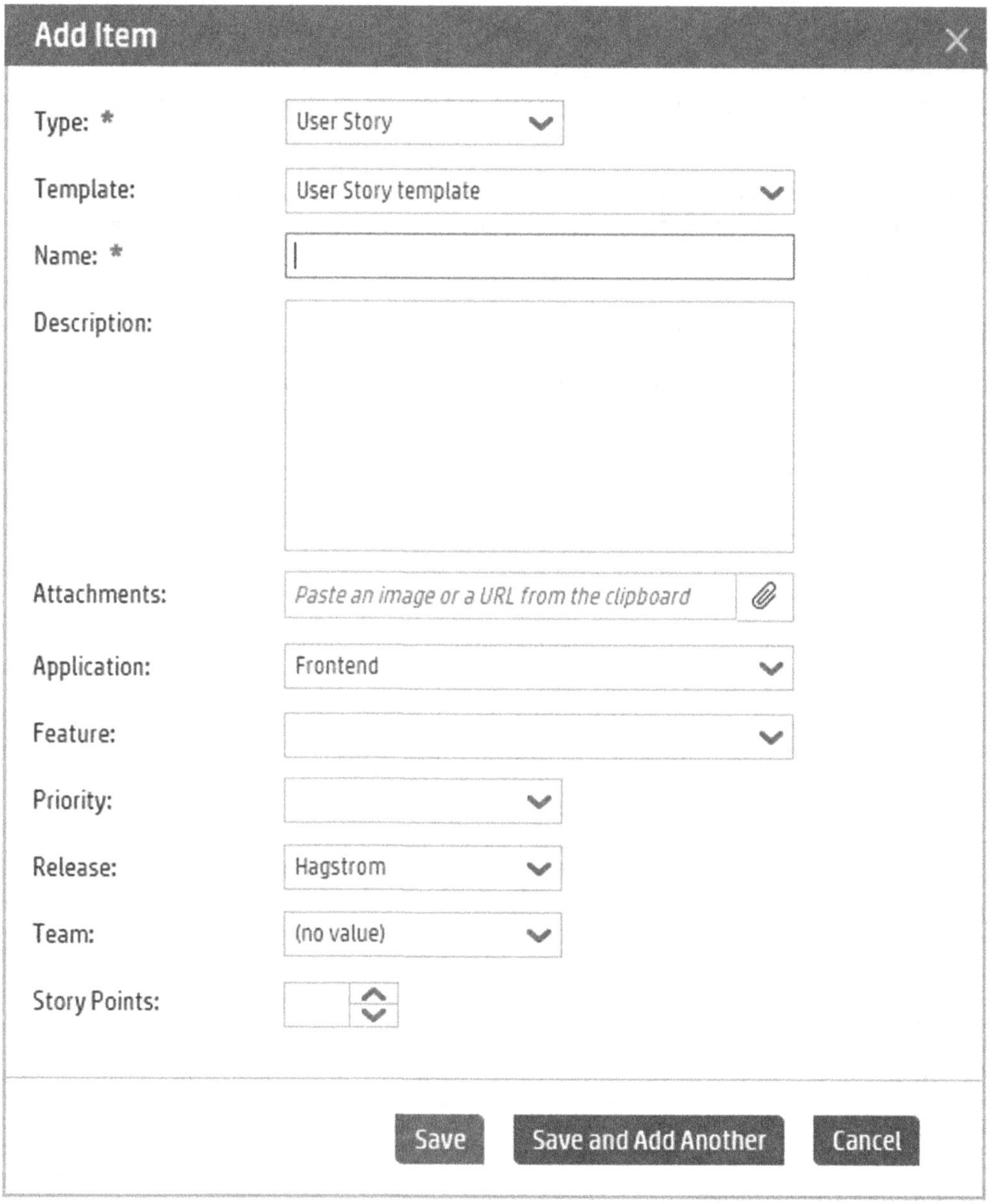

Figure 5-2. *Adding a user story*

73

Enter **As a user, I would like to subscribe to notifications when new content is available** as the name for the user story (in practice, this should be considered as content for the user story description), and although this is the only required field to create a user story (besides the type, which is prepopulated already), it allows you to set other useful fields at this time: Description, Attachments, Feature, Application, Priority, and Story Points. Set these fields accordingly with values available from previous chapters, as well as the Release and Team fields. Also notice the Template field, which allows you to choose from a user story or a defect template that you created previously in the configuration area when setting up Agile Manager.

■ **Note**   It is possible to place a picture in the Attachments field by making a copy of the image using the Copy Image option in the browser's right-click context menu or by copying it to the clipboard and then pressing the Ctrl+V or Ctrl+Insert keys while the cursor is in the Attachments field. This provides a quick way to add an image as an attachment to any backlog item, without needing to store and save the image locally on your desktop.

After populating the fields and clicking the Save button, the user story will be added to the current release backlog and to the current sprint because you're on the Sprint Backlog page. The grid layout will refresh, and the new user story that you added will also be selected and highlighted.

Viewing and Editing a User Story

For the user story you just added, let's click its ID value in the ID column to edit and view the user story's details, as shown in Figure 5-3. You'll begin by reviewing the sections that the user story consists of.

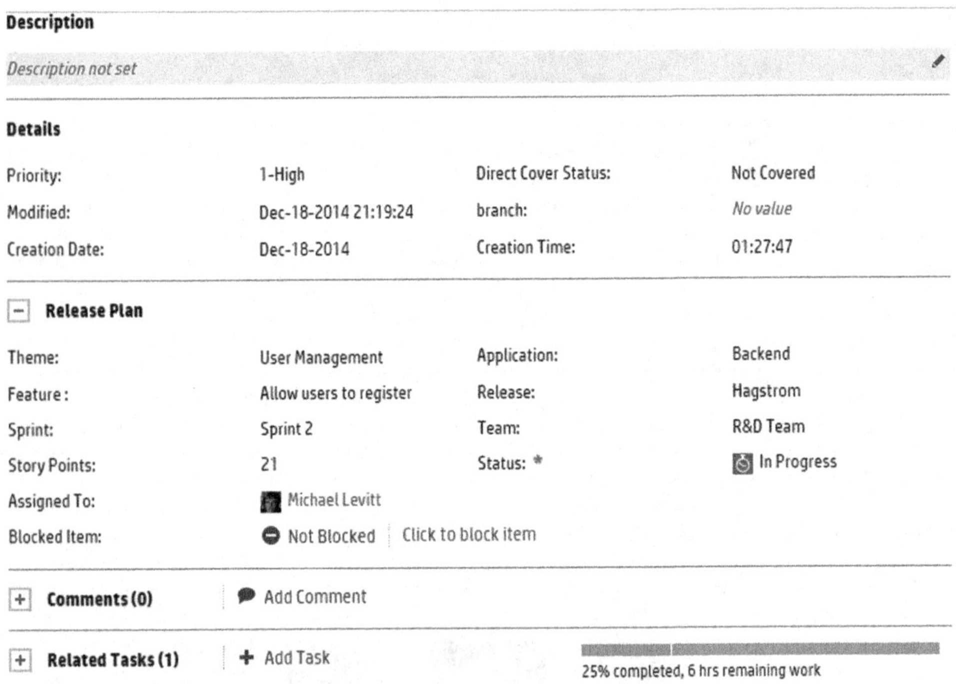

Description

Description not set ✎

Details

Priority:	1–High	Direct Cover Status:	Not Covered
Modified:	Dec-18-2014 21:19:24	branch:	No value
Creation Date:	Dec-18-2014	Creation Time:	01:27:47

[−] **Release Plan**

Theme:	User Management	Application:	Backend
Feature :	Allow users to register	Release:	Hagstrom
Sprint:	Sprint 2	Team:	R&D Team
Story Points:	21	Status: *	⊙ In Progress
Assigned To:	▨ Michael Levitt		
Blocked Item:	⊖ Not Blocked Click to block item		

[+] **Comments (0)**   💬 Add Comment

[+] **Related Tasks (1)**   ✚ Add Task

25% completed, 6 hrs remaining work

Figure 5-3. *User story's section details*

The Description section puts the user story information at the top of the center content panel, and even though a user story's description is often treated as not being longer than text you could put on an A4 notecard, this section features a WYSIWYG field that allows you to place rich-text markup and paste content from Microsoft Word.

The Details section displays metadata information about the user story, such as Creation Date, Modified, and other fields.

■ **Note**   Agile Manager allows you to add up to five custom fields to a user story or defect backlog item. When these are added, they will show up in the Details section of the backlog item.

The Release Plan section includes all the details concerned with the backlog item's association for the release, such as the feature it belongs to (which sets the Theme field automatically), sprint, application, release, and team information. It also includes the user story's status, Story Points setting, and an Assign To field to assign the item to a member of the team.

■ **Note**   Agile Manager's user interface allows for the autocompletion of text for most of the drop-down selection fields. For example, clicking the Feature field will list the available themes and features, and typing any text in the input field will filter the listed results.

When viewing a user story or other backlog item that was opened from the grid listing, the item will feature a contextual navigation button at the top right of the page, as shown in Figure 5-4. This button allows you to move forward and backward through backlog items in the grid listing, whether it was filtered or not, and view each item.

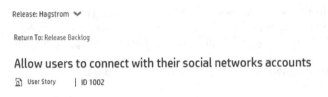

Figure 5-4. *User story's backlog navigation*

The Return To link in the top left of the page allows you to switch back to the grid listing from which the current backlog item was opened and maintains any filters and settings of the grid layout.

Adding Comments

Just like with features and themes, user stories and defects enable communication and collaboration through the commenting capability. Comments can be added by clicking the Add Comment button, and you will be presented with the Add New Comment pop-up dialog shown in Figure 5-5 to add rich text.

Figure 5-5. *User story's comments*

▪ **Note** In the current version, at the time of writing this book, Agile Manager doesn't allow you to edit or remove comments. All comments are added and displayed.

Adding Tasks

Tasks for user stories or defects enable you to sum up the effort required for the item in measures of work and are estimated in hours. Tasks are great for breaking down a user story into smaller units of work that don't tend to convert to user stories. The following are examples of tasks that are great places for adding R&D effort:

- Adding unit tests
- Adding acceptance tests
- Adding cross-browser support
- Performing code reviews

Figure 5-6 shows how to add a task. Simply click the Add Task button. In the Add New Task pop-up dialog, the Assignee field will already be set to the team member who this item is assigned to, or if that's not set, the field will default to no value. For scoping the work effort required in this task, the Estimated (Hours) field will default to the value set in the configuration area per this workspace.

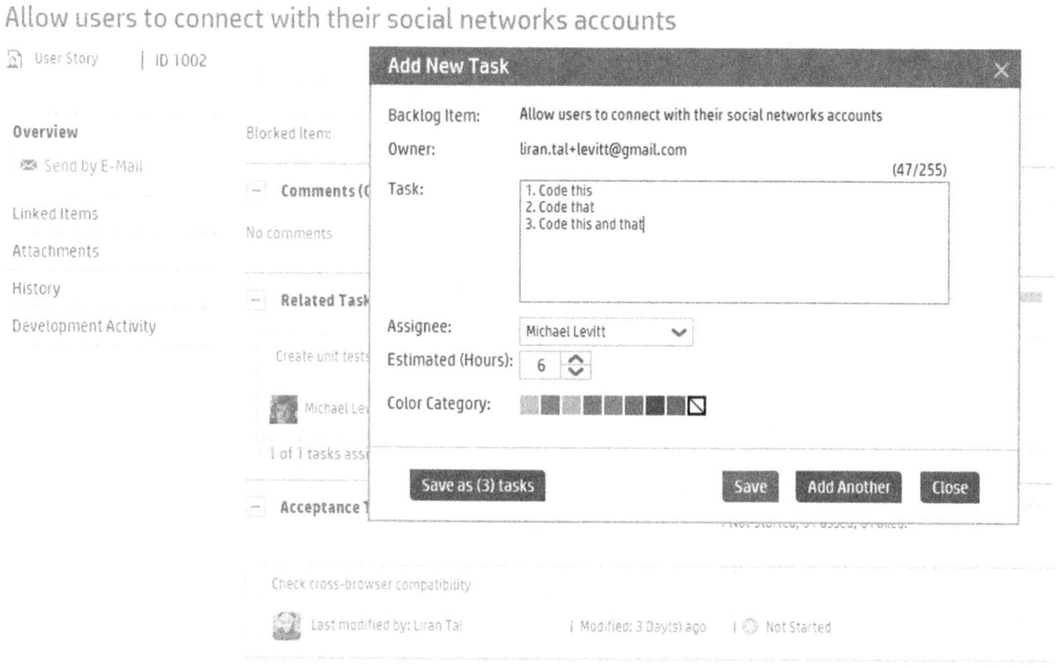

Figure 5-6. User story's tasks

■ **Note** If you are using bullets or numbering in the task description, Agile Manager will detect this and allow you to create multiple tasks, as shown in the "Save as (3) tasks" button at the bottom left of Figure 5-6.

By selecting a color category, it is possible to differentiate tasks when viewing them in the tasks list or on other pages such as the Task Board page. It is good practice to use color defaults when setting up the tasks to make it easy to differentiate development, quality assurance, and documentation tasks.

Adding Acceptance Tests

Unlike other backlog items in Agile Manager, only user stories feature the capability of tracking acceptance tests.

Acceptance tests for user stories, while not tied to an automated test runner, allow you to tell the QA department where to concentrate effort. This also is good practice for the user story owner to conform with a few rules before closing the user story and setting it to Done. QA testers can also be involved in the process of creating a user story and suggest various acceptance tests to be added.

To create a new acceptance test, as shown in Figure 5-7, click Add Acceptance Test and provide the test description, up to 555 characters long, which helps ensure that tests are well explained. The Status field will default to Not Started, yet when the user story is being tested, QA can set the Acceptance Test status to Passed or Failed, which helps indicate where the user story failed.

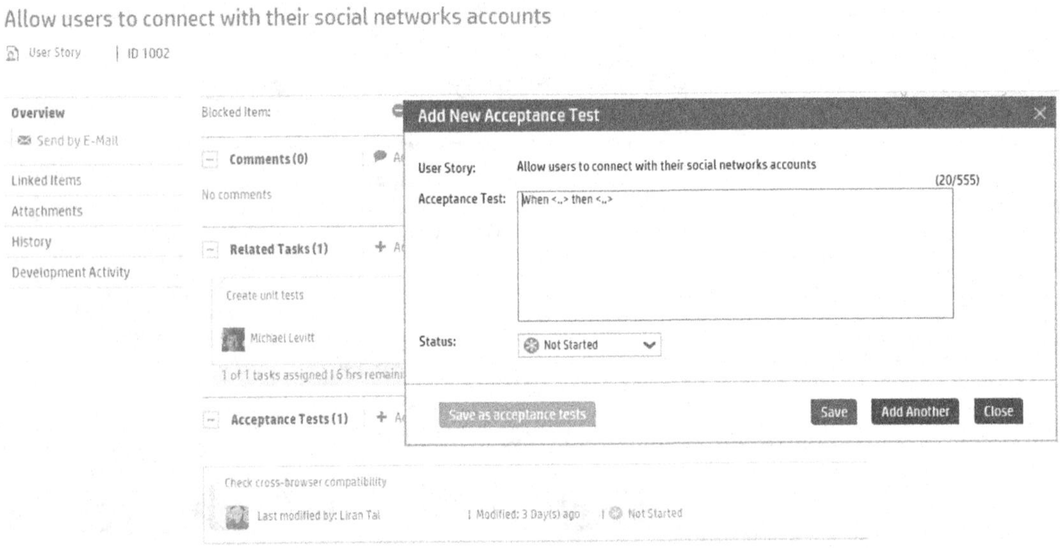

Figure 5-7. *User story's acceptance tests*

Auditing User Stories

Agile Manager implements an auditing mechanism for backlog items, which helps you track the history of the item as it changes. This capability is useful when a status changes and you need to investigate when this changed and who changed it. This is crucial because Agile Manager's advanced user interface features such as drag-and-drop functionality will change a backlog item's details behind the scenes and may not always be obvious.

To track the history of backlog items, click History in the left sidebar panel, which will reveal auditing information, meaning the Old Value and New Value settings. Each change is also timestamped and logs the user who performed the change, as shown in Figure 5-8.

Allow users to connect with their social networks accounts

🗐 User Story　|　ID 1002

Overview	Filter By Changer All ⌄　Field Name All ⌄	
Linked Items	**Field Name**　　Old Value	**New Value**
Attachments	▸ Time: Dec-18-2014 21:19:25 (1 Field) Changer: liran.tal@gmail.com	
History	▸ Time: Dec-18-2014 21:18:56 (2 Fields) Changer: liran.tal@gmail.com	
Development Activity	▸ Time: Dec-18-2014 04:53:38 (2 Fields) Changer: liran.tal@gmail.com	
	▸ Time: Dec-18-2014 04:17:18 (1 Field) Changer: liran.tal@gmail.com	
	▾ Time: Dec-18-2014 04:16:49 (3 Fields) Changer: liran.tal@gmail.com	
	Lane	New
	Sprint	Sprint 2
	Team	R&D Team
	▾ Time: Dec-18-2014 01:27:48 (3 Fields) Changer: liran.tal@gmail.com	
	Priority	1-High
	Release	Hagstrom
	Application	Backend
	12 Changes	

Figure 5-8. *User story's auditing*

When the auditing history grows, it is possible to apply some filters to search for the relevant change, such as by using the Filter By Changer to see the user who performed this change or to track a specific field change using the Field Name filter.

Working in the Sprint Backlog

While backlog items such as user stories can be added in the both the release backlog and the sprint backlog, it is generally best practice for the team to work in the context of the sprint backlog because it consolidates and focuses the relevant backlog items for the current sprint the team is on.

Let's review some of the sprint-related information available when viewing the Sprint Backlog page.

Contextual Filters

The Sprint Backlog page, as shown in Figure 5-9, makes the following contextual filters available, in addition to the Release and Application filters.

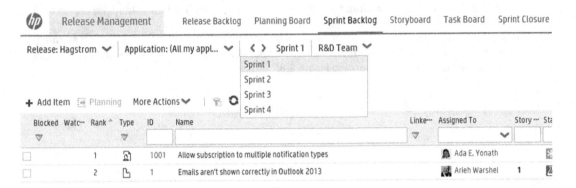

Figure 5-9. *The Sprint Backlog page's contextual filters*

- *Sprint selection*: A contextual filter to show backlog items for the current sprint or a desired sprint. It is possible to navigate back and forth between sprints or choose a specific sprint.

- *Team selection*: A contextual filter to toggle between backlog items assigned to different teams.

Sprint Widgets

Visual representation of the sprint status is made available through the widgets at the top right of the screen, as shown in Figure 5-10.

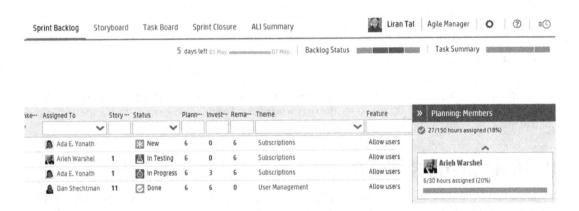

Figure 5-10. *The sprint backlog status widgets*

- *Sprint timeline*: A visual widget for showing the current sprint timeline you're on, as well as the days left for the current sprint.

- *Sprint status*: Uses two visual widgets to show a big-picture representation of the current sprint; the Backlog Status widget will show the status distribution of backlog items, and the Task Summary widget will show the status of tasks for both user stories and defects.

Sprint Panels

With regard to panels available in the Sprint Backlog page, the filter and grouping panel that you're familiar with in the right sidebar isn't available, but as shown in Figure 5-11, two other panels are made available.

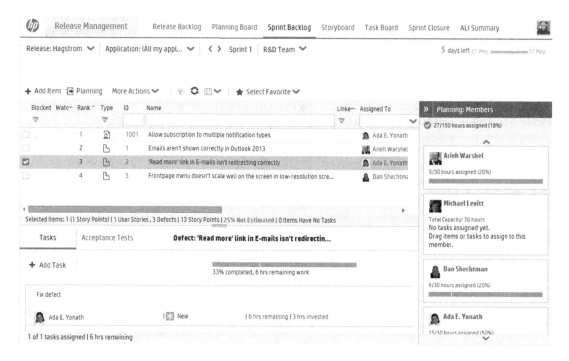

Figure 5-11. *The Sprint Backlog page*

- *Planning: Members panel*: In the right sidebar, you'll be able to view each team member's capacity. This information is useful when coupled with work hour estimations set on backlog items to understand whether a team member is overloaded with work for the current sprint or has enough capacity to do all the work assigned.

- *Tasks and Acceptance Tests panel*: When selecting a user story or defect, the bottom panel will provide quick access to the backlog item's subitems such as tasks and acceptance tests (except for defects, which has no acceptance tests). It is also possible to quickly add tasks for defects or stories from this panel or update existing task settings.

- *Status bar*: The bottom status bar summarizes the number of user stories, the number of defects, the aggregated sum of story points for all backlog items, the task count, and the percent of backlog items that are not estimated (which acts as a link that can be toggled on and off to switch between items that are estimated and that aren't).

■ **Note**   The status bar allows you to get hints on the filters that are applied to the current grid listing by hovering over the gray gear-shaped icon at the beginning of the status bar information.

Grid Layout

Since you will mostly be busy working with items in the grid, it is important to learn how to interact with the grid layout to speed up your work.

Selecting multiple items in the grid is often useful, and instead of selecting the check boxes for each item in the grid listing, you can select the first item from the list and then select the last item while holding the Shift key. The result will be that all items from the first to the last are selected.

In every grid layout, you can right-click backlog items to open a contextual item menu, as shown in Figure 5-12. This reveals actions that can be performed on the currently selected backlog item.

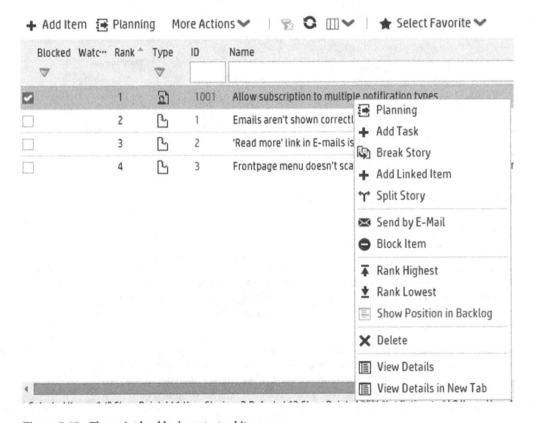

Figure 5-12. *The sprint backlog's contextual item menu*

Managing and Viewing a Member's Sprint Capacity

Figure 5-13 shows the Planning: Members panel in the right sidebar, which is useful for understanding the team capacity for the sprint and figuring out whether an individual team member is overloaded with tasks or can take on more items to work on.

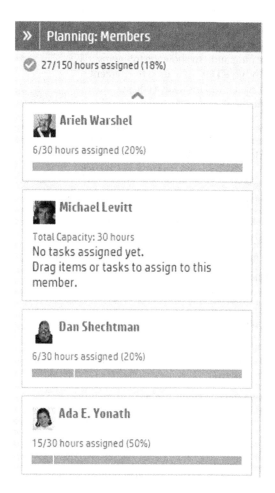

Figure 5-13. *The sprint capacity planning for team members*

When the Sprint Backlog page loads, the Planning: Members panel will automatically be populated and refreshed with all team members for the configured team contextual filter setting.

■ **Note**   The Planning: Members panel indicates a member's capacity based on hours of work units, as set for their tasks in the backlog items. By default, Agile Manager allots six hours of work per day for each team member.

Let's review the information available through in the Planning: Members panel.

- *Team member*: Each team member block begins with their clickable name heading and picture thumbnail. When this heading is clicked, the grid layout filters the listing to show only the items assigned to this team member.

- *Member capacity*: This shows the hours assigned out of the total hours available for each team member as a capacity indicator for the current sprint.

- *Member capacity bar*: In addition to the numbers data, which shows the member's capacity, the capacity bar also provides a visual indication to show the following available status indicators: gray for total capacity, green for indicating the percent of work done, and blue for the remaining work, which will indicate a correct value because it is relative to the timeline of the sprint.

Team members with no tasks assigned will simply have the total available capacity displayed with some text noting that no tasks are assigned; members who are over capacity will show up with a red *x* icon, and the progress bar will use red to show the percentage of the overloaded work for the team member.

▪ **Note**　When working with the Capacity Planning panel on the Sprint Backlog page, it is important to notice that the available capacity isn't relative to the current time of the sprint. Meaning, it's possible that you will be in the last day of the sprint, and the available capacity will show up 100 percent because a team member isn't assigned any tasks. Obviously, that will be false because the available capacity is only six hours if you're using Agile Manager's defaults for a member's capacity where six hours is the daily capacity.

As shown in Figure 5-14, the Capacity Planning panel allows further interaction:

- *Assign backlog items*: By dragging sprint backlog items from the grid layout to a team member's capacity block, it is possible to automatically set that member as the owner of that item, as well as assigning all tasks to them.

- *Adjust member capacity*: By clicking the capacity information link in each member's capacity block, it is possible to adjust the number of working days in a sprint, along with the number of hours per day per sprint.

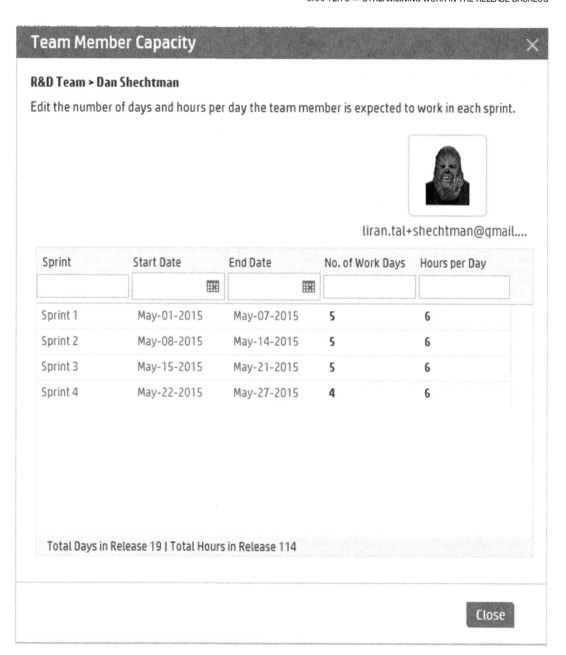

Figure 5-14. *The sprint team member capacity*

Actions in the Grid Toolbar

The actions available in the grid toolbar vary on different pages. Let's review the commonly available actions for backlog items and specifically for user stories in the grid toolbar.

Planning

If you want to change items and assign them to a different release, sprint, or team, then simply toggle one or more backlog items from the grid listing so that they are selected and click the Planning option in the grid toolbar to set the fields accordingly, as shown in Figure 5-15.

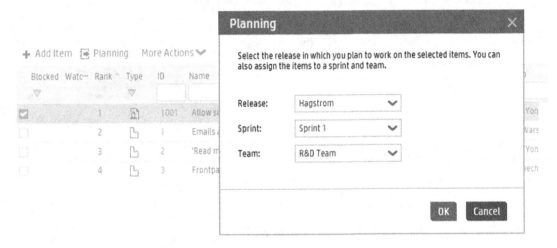

Figure 5-15. *The Sprint Backlog page's Planning pop-up*

Bulk Updating Items

The grid layout makes updating a backlog item a breeze with inline editing available for most columns in the grid; you simply click an item and set a new value. It is, however, another story when you want to update more than one item with the same value.

To bulk update any items, toggle them in the grid layout, and from the grid toolbar click More Actions ➤ Update Selected. In the pop-up dialog, as shown in Figure 5-16, click Add Property to choose fields that need to be updated and then set their values accordingly. Once you're done, click the Update button to apply the bulk update action.

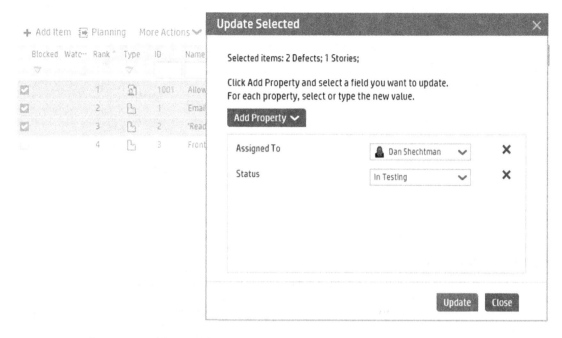

Figure 5-16. The Sprint Backlog page: bulk updating

Blocking a User Story or Defect

Sometimes when working on implementing a user story or fixing a defect, there may be external constraints that you are dependent upon to complete the item or even local issues such as a team member not pushing related code so your implementation has to be stalled and can't be completed or tested correctly.

To meet this kind of incomplete user story, Agile Manager provides the ability to block items with a given reason, until the constraint is cleared, upon which time the issue can be easily unblocked.

▥ **Note**   Blocking or unblocking an item is merely a metadata attribute on a backlog item and does not enforce or include any automatic tools to process this mode.

To block items, toggle them in the grid layout so they are selected and click More Actions ➤ Block Item. The pop-up dialog, as shown in Figure 5-17, will request you to provide a reason for blocking the items. When you're done, click Finish. Blocked items will then show up with a red "no access" icon in the grid layout and when viewing them individually.

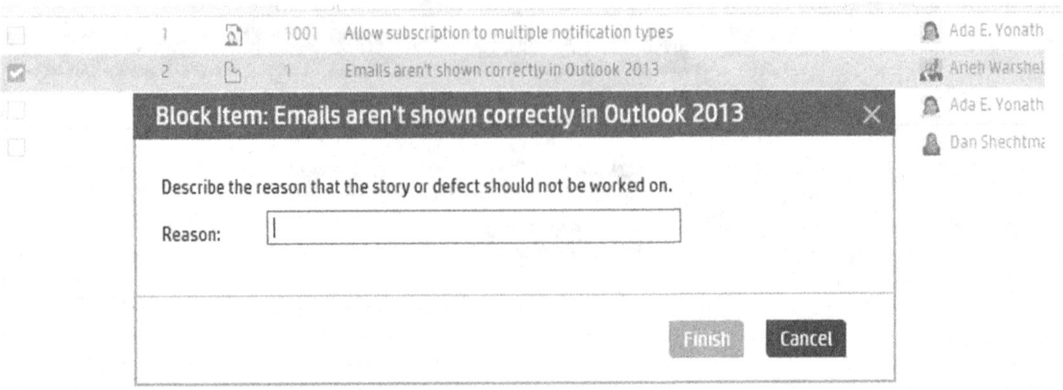

Figure 5-17. *The Sprint Backlog page: blocked items*

Splitting a User Story

If at the end of a sprint a story can't be closed, it can be split so that remaining tasks can be moved on to a new user story in the next sprint.

To split a story, toggle the story in the grid layout so it is selected, and click More Actions ➤ Split Story. The pop-up dialog, as shown in Figure 5-18, prefills the "New story name" field with some postfix text to note the continuation of this user story based on a previous one. Planning-wise, the new story will already be assigned to the next sprint, as the "New story planned sprint" field shows.

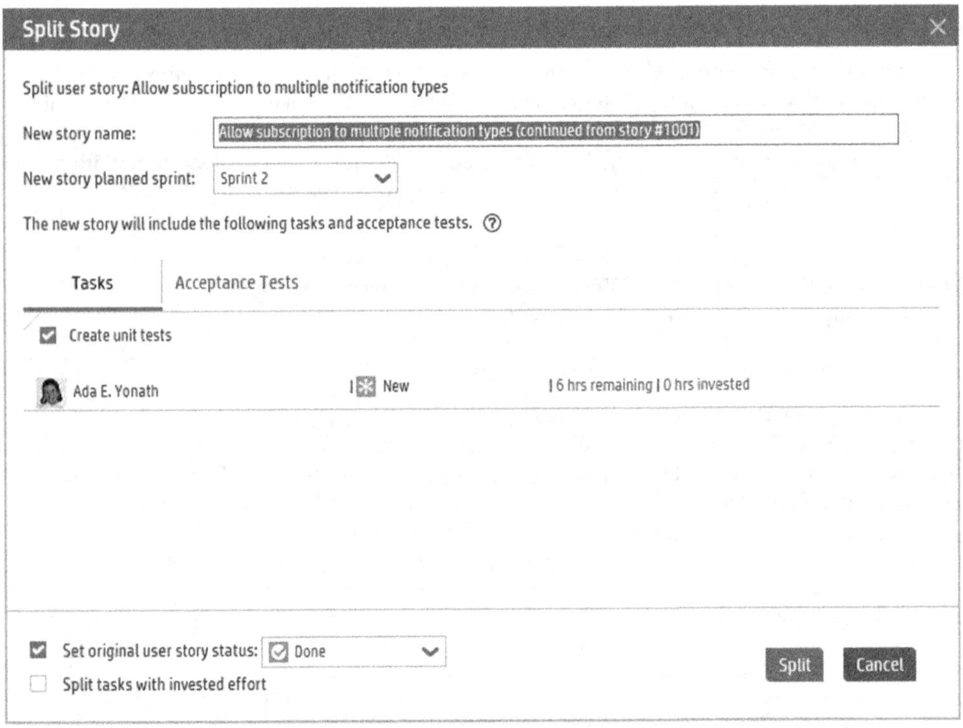

Figure 5-18. *The Sprint Backlog: splitting a user story*

All tasks that are incomplete and acceptance tests that did not pass will be moved out from the current user story that is split to the new one that is being created. By toggling the "Set original user story status" option, the current user story can remain in an In-Testing status, so it is still passed to the QA team or simply moved to a Done status.

Once you're done setting the story up, click the Split button to create the new story.

Sending Item Notifications

Even though Agile Manager supports notification triggers such as when user is assigned an item, it is often required to send out a reminder for an item or to send a general e-mail about a backlog item.

To send an item, click More Actions ➤ Send by E-Mail. The pop-up dialog, as shown in Figure 5-19, will show the compose e-mail form; you should add the recipients, set the subject, and add a message. Then send it by clicking the Send button.

Figure 5-19. *The Sprint Backlog page: sending item by e-mail*

■ **Note** Only users of the currently selected workspace can be sent an e-mail. Users with a general e-mail address such as @gmail.com or @yahoo.com aren't valid recipients.

It is possible to send yourself a copy of the e-mail by selecting the "Send me a copy" option or to select "Include attachments" to make sure the e-mail contains any attached resources on the backlog item.

■ **Note** When multiple backlog items are selected to be sent by e-mail, each item will be sent and received as a single email.

Managing Defects

Filing defects, tracking them, and managing them are common tasks for any software development project, and Agile Manager has an entire section just for managing defects.

Defects can be created like any other backlog item, through the common Add Item option on the grid toolbar that you've seen more than a few times. While on the Release Management and Sprint Backlog pages, this option defaults to user story creation. It is simply a matter of choosing to create a defect as the backlog item type.

To start working with defects, click Defect Management in the top navigation area, which will open the corresponding page for managing defects, as shown in Figure 5-20.

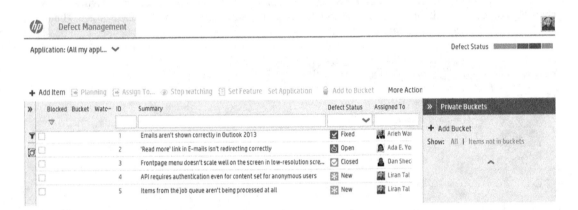

Figure 5-20. *Defect management*

Adding Defects

Let's begin by adding a few defects to the product backlog by clicking the Add Item option in the grid toolbar. The Add New Defect pop-up dialog, as shown in Figure 5-21, will set the default defects template and allow you to add a defect summary, reproduce the methodology through the Description field, add any resource as attachments, and state the severity of the defect as a required field.

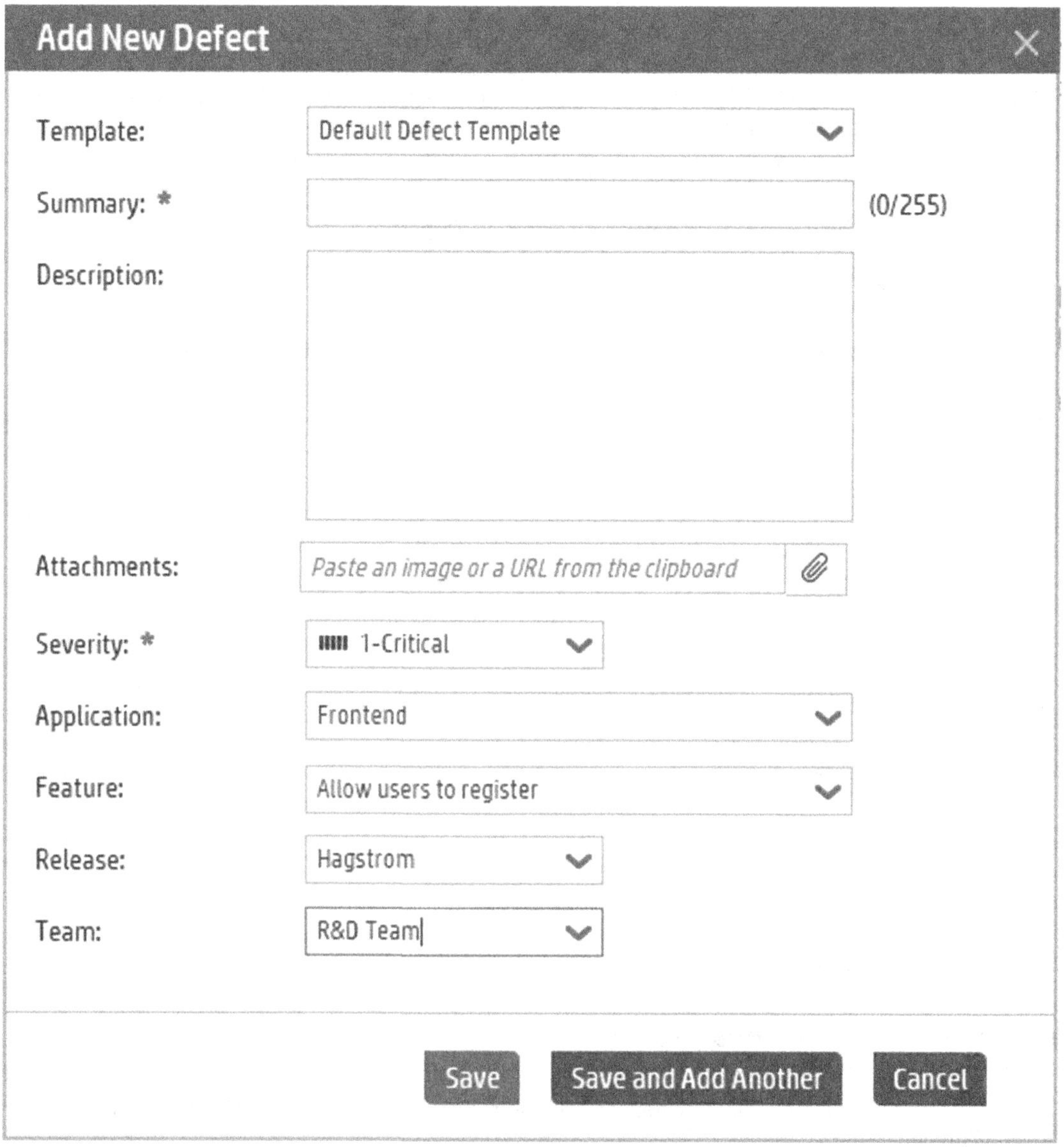

Figure 5-21. *Defect management: adding a new defect*

▪ **Note** When defects are added, it's a good practice to also set their relevant feature and application because these values should be known at the time of reporting the defect. This will also make it possible to view user stories and defects that are related to the same feature when viewed on the Sprint Backlog page, Release Backlog page, or other pages such as the Dashboard page.

Once you are satisfied with the defect details, click Save or Save and Add Another to save and continue working in the defect management area.

Editing Defects

To view a defect and edit its settings, let's click the ID value in the grid listing. The defect view page, as shown in Figure 5-22, will open. Quite similar to user stories' edit and view pages, defects share common fields but provide more defect-related properties.

- *Defect Status*: Unlike user stories that have a Status field to denote the state of the item, defects have specific fields for denoting the status of the defect itself, not just the state, such as Fixed, Propose Close, Deferred, Duplicate, Rejected, and others.

- *Closed, and Fixed on Date*: These will automatically be set when Defect Status is set to Fixed and when the Status field is updated to Done.

- *Severity*: Defects that criticality impact the application can be set to anything from Low to Critical.

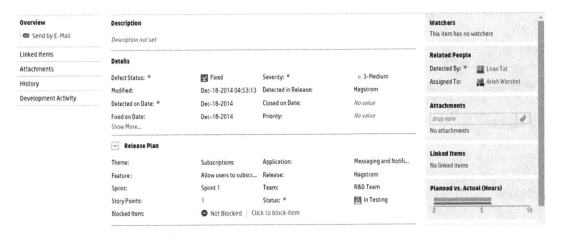

Figure 5-22. *Defect management: editing a defect*

Defects have in common other functionality with user stories, such as the commenting, tasks, attachments, and history.

Linking Defects

Linking defects to user stories and associating them with each other has several benefits, most importantly the following:

- *Visibility*: When defects are assigned to user stories, this will allow for both QA and developers to easily find all defects that are related to a user story and need fixing, as well as providing information on the quality of the user story with ease.

- *Enforcing workflow*: You saw in Chapter 3 how to set up workspace settings, and specifically you learned how it's possible to restrict a user story to move into the Done status only when all associated defects are fixed. By employing the methodology of linking defects to user stories, this workflow can be enforced and practiced.

■ **Note**   Defects can be linked to other defects too.

Let's click the defect IDs in the grid listing for any of the defects that you've just added and link the defects to a user story. In the defects view, click the Linked Items option in the left sidebar to open the linked items page. Click Link to User Stories, and a pop-up dialog with a lightweight grid will show up, as shown in Figure 5-23. Here you can search for the relevant user story to link to. Select the stories to select them, and click the OK button to apply.

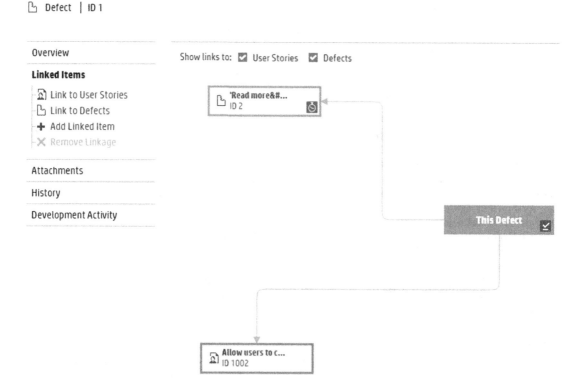

Figure 5-23. *Defect management: linking defects*

The default linked items page will show the links through the items in the Diagram view, but the Grid view can also be switched on by using the top-right buttons in the links panel.

Watching Backlog Items

Along with the manual trigger for e-mail notifications, which is available through the Send By E-mail action on every backlog item, Agile Manager allows you to subscribe to notifications on specific events and automatically get e-mail messages when changes occur to backlog items.

When watching items, in the event of a status change to the backlog item, all users who are set to watch the item will receive the e-mail notification.

To begin watching items while in the Defect Management area, select any defect in the listed items; then locate the Watch action on the grid toolbar and click it. After doing so, a status message will show up at the top of the page, as shown in Figure 5-24, to indicate that the action took place. From that point on, you will receive e-mail notifications for changes happening on any of the defect items you are set to watch.

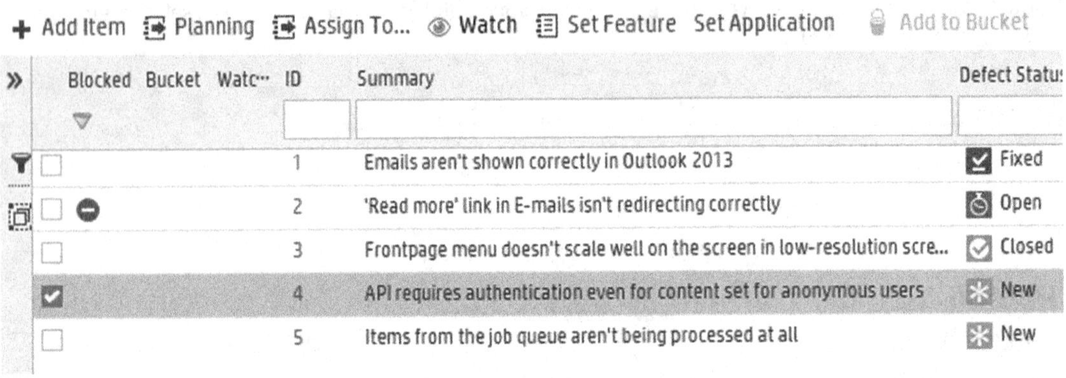

Figure 5-24. *Defect management: watching items*

It is also possible to assign other users to watch a defect for updates. To do so, click the More Actions options in the grid toolbar, and select the Add Watcher action from the drop-down list. This will pop up the Select User dialog and will prompt you to select a user from a list to apply the watch setting for.

As shown in Figure 5-25, the backlog item page shows the users who are watching it. To investigate that information for the defect items you've just set to watch, click the defect item in the grid layout listing to go to the defect's view page. The backlog item will then show the Watchers block in the right sidebar; it shows up at the top. In this case, it shows just the user as the watcher for this defect.

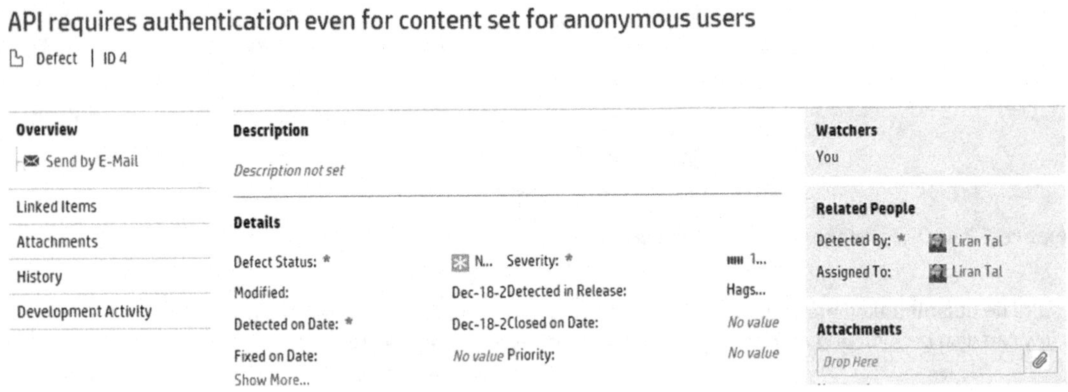

Figure 5-25. *Defect management: item watch list*

For better visibility of watched items, as well as being able to stop watching an item, it is required to add the Watched column field to the grid layout. To do that, click the icon resembeling a table's column layout to add a new column field to the grid display, and from the list choose the Watched field. Once selected, it will be added as the last column on the grid, so to make it easier to follow, drag and drop the column from the end of the grid display to the start.

Once the Watched field is added to the grid display, any backlog items that are watched will show up with a gray eye icon, as shown in Figure 5-26. When the item is selected, it will now also be possible to choose the "Stop watching" action from the grid toolbar to stop notifications for the selected backlog items.

	Blocked	Bucket	Watc⋯	ID	Summary		Defect Status
	☐			1	Emails aren't shown correctly in Outlook 2013		☑ Fixed
	☐	⊖		2	'Read more' link in E-mails isn't redirecting correctly		◉ Open
	☐			3	Frontpage menu doesn't scale well on the screen in low-resolution scre...		☑ Closed
	☐		◉	4	API requires authentication even for content set for anonymous users		✳ New
	☑		◉	5	Items from the job queue aren't being processed at all		✳ New

Toolbar: ✚ Add Item   ▣ Planning   ▣ Assign To...   ◉ Stop watching   ▤ Set Feature   Set Application   🗑 Add to Bucket

Figure 5-26. *Defect management: watched items list in grid display*

Working in the Sprint Closure

When ending a sprint or a release, it is a common agile practice to have a sprint retrospective. During the sprint retrospective meeting, the team reviews how things went, gauges metrics for the sprint to review, and can take action items to further improve in future sprints or releases.

Agile Manager facilitates this process using the Sprint Closure page in the Release Management area. In the upper part of the page, several widgets are available that present sprint summary metrics for the team to review, and the lower part of the page enables the recording of things that went well and the things to improve; it is a common agile practice to transparently share information across the team in a retrospective meeting and to create action items for future improvement.

Sprint Backlog Status

An overall view of user stories and defects from the backlog is presented in this widget, as shown in Figure 5-27. It shows the amount of completed items by the team and adds in the QA team to the session by showing the detected defects; it also indicates the build health status if Agile Manager is connected to a source code versioning system and build automation tools such as Jenkins or Travis.

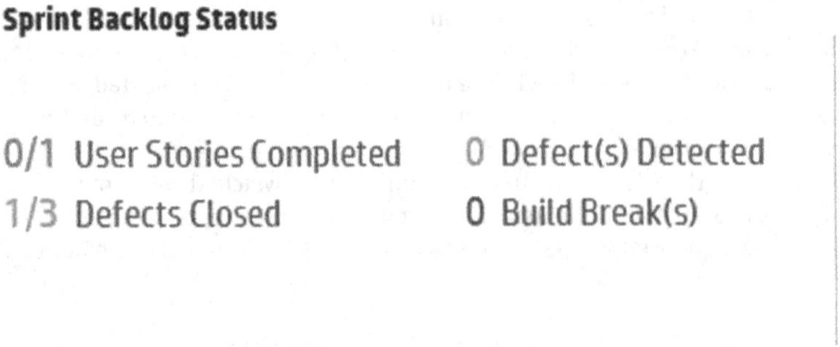

Sprint Backlog Status

0/1 User Stories Completed   0 Defect(s) Detected

1/3 Defects Closed   0 Build Break(s)

Figure 5-27. Sprint retrospective backlog status

Backlog Planning and Delivery

The Backlog Planning and Delivery widget, as shown in Figure 5-28, enables a retrospective on the sprint planning process; it shows two columns, Planned and Added, for user stories, and it is possible to tell the number of stories that were added during the sprint.

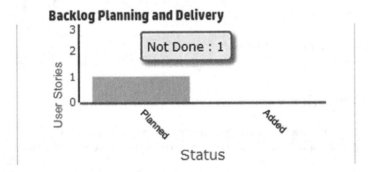

Figure 5-28. Sprint retrospective backlog status

The graph indicates the number of user stories set to Done versus those set to Not Done. All stories that are considered Not Done are those that are set to either New, In Progress, or In Testing.

You can tell from this graph that many of the user stories that were planned are still not done, which may mean they have been finished by developers but are still waiting for QA with the In Testing status; you can also see that many user stories (almost the same number as those that were planned) were added during the sprint.

Defect Cumulative Flow Diagram

As shown in Figure 5-29, this widget shows the defects count and their status changes throughout the release.

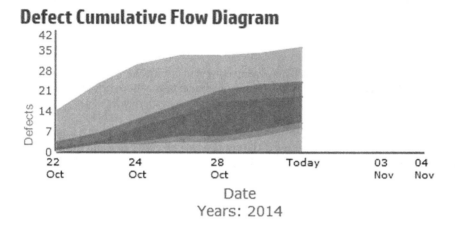

Figure 5-29. *Sprint retrospective defects status*

Here are some insights to gain from this widget:

- A higher fixed, closed defects ratio to items in new is better.

- Preferably new defects will show a rise at first, and then the curve should slow down to a minimum as no defects are found. If new defects are still being found at a high rate toward the end of the sprint, then there's bigger risk for low-quality code or features, which indicates the project is not stable.

Acceptance Tests

Figure 5-30 shows a simple yet effective widget that displays the number of tests passed or failed and those that have not been started. These tests are of course not related to any automated acceptance tests but are rather the set of tests that developers and QA defined in their user stories as initial input and expected actual results when testing a user story.

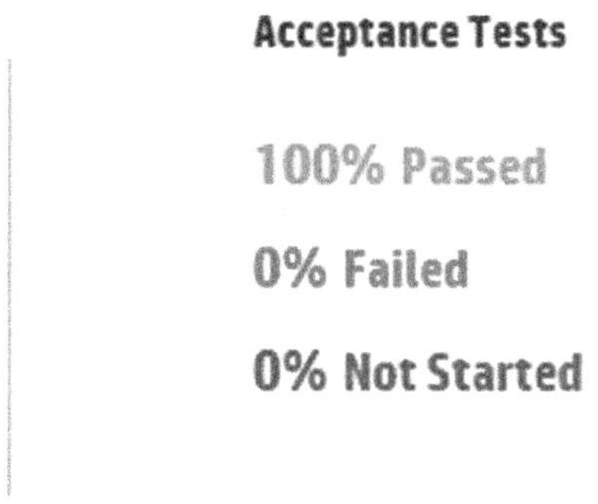

Acceptance Tests

100% Passed

0% Failed

0% Not Started

Figure 5-30. *Sprint retrospective acceptance tests status*

▪ **Note** The Sprint Closure page is always available, even in the middle of the sprint, and is always up-to-date with the backlog items' status for the sprint. Therefore, it is a good tool to show where the team stands during the sprint so that there are no surprises when completing it.

Retrospective Feedback

As is common in agile practices, the focus of a retrospective meeting is to discuss the sprint with the team. This discussion isn't limited to just testers and developers but is a broader look at how the team executed in general, including other functions such as the collaboration with the user experience (UX) expert, the functional architect (FA), team leaders, and so on.

To facilitate this discussion, Agile Manager provides a text field to record those things that went well, as well as those things to improve, as shown in Figure 5-31. The entire team can participate and share their own perspectives in a transparent manner.

Things that went well

> List the things that worked well for the team during the sprint

➲ Convert to 0 action item(s)

Things to improve

> List the things that can be improved in future sprints

➲ Convert to 0 action item(s)

Figure 5-31. *Sprint retrospective feedback*

Items added to any of the previous inputs can be further tracked by creating action items for them, and Agile Manager will automatically detect bulleted or numbered items and prompt you to convert them to action items.

■ **Note**   As the input from the team is recorded in the text fields, it is also saved to Agile Manager, and no further action such as clicking a Save button is required.

When action items are specified, they can be assigned to all team members or to a specific team member. They can also be converted to a user story, so clicking the Create User Story action will pop up the Add Item dialog to add a story backlog item.

Action items can also be ranked in terms of priorities by moving them up or down in the list or by completely removing them.

As shown in Figure 5-32, when sprint retrospectives are revisited to review the action items, they can then be toggled as Done to indicate that action items are indeed being followed up on.

Figure 5-32. Sprint retrospective action items

■ **Note**   At the right-bottom side of the Sprint Closure page, you might have noticed a tab that can be expanded to the left side of the page with a label of "Open item(s)." Once clicked and expanded, this tab will present the grid layout with the list of all open items (as well as those that are set to In Testing status), and as common with sprint retrospectives, these items will need to be moved to the next sprint, if existing, or elsewhere such as the product backlog, depending on the decision of the team.

Summary

In this chapter, you learned how sprints are handled with Agile Manager, and specifically you reviewed the way user stories and defects are managed throughout a sprint. You also learned how the sprint retrospective process is facilitated using the Sprint Closure page and how further action items and sprint metrics are useful to continually monitor the status of the sprint.

■ ■ ■

CHAPTER 6

The Engineering Manager's Dashboard

Now that you know your way through Agile Manager and have learned how to plan your product backlog and your release backlog, it is essential to track the progress of releases and sprints to move in an agile way and diminish any unplanned surprises.

In this chapter, you'll learn how to harness the power of dashboards, widgets, and metrics in Agile Manager to track your progress, whether you are a manager or a developer. We'll cover the following topics:

- Using Agile Manager's Dashboard view

- Adding and customizing the dashboard

- Creating your own widgets

- Tips on using essential widgets to track release and sprint progress

Working in the Dashboard

Whereas in previous chapters you learned how to manage the release cycle from start to end, it is crucial that everyone always be able to track the release cycle and status of all of their defects, stories, and backlog items in general.

The Dashboard view is packed with configurable and customizable widgets and a layouts view, which is all about gaining insight on a research and development (R&D) team member's status.

To view and manage the Dashboard view shown in Figure 6-1, click the Dashboard option in the main navigation bar.

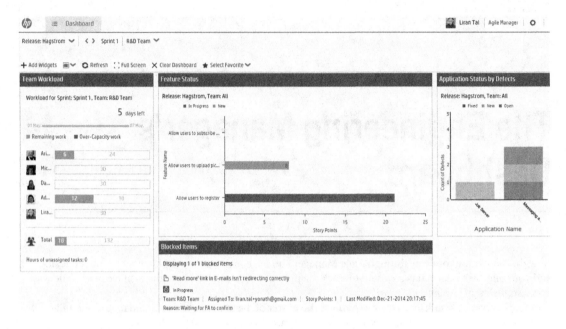

Figure 6-1. *Dashboard view*

As with other areas that we've covered so far, the dashboard has contextual filters that allow you to zoom in on specific releases, sprints, and teams as required. Switching between these options allows you to easily see the overall status of any component because the widgets refresh automatically.

Dashboard Layouts

By default, Agile Manager offers a few widget configuration layouts, depending on the role of the user.

- *Developer dashboard*: This is a widget collection for developers and quality assurance engineers; it includes My Defects, My Stories, My Watched Defects, and Defects Detected by Me.

- *Kanban dashboard*: This is a widget collection for Scrum masters or product owners who want to track a Kanban-based release through widgets; it includes Release Control Chart, Average Cycle Time, and Storyboard Cumulative Flow.

- *Release Manager dashboard*: This is a widget collection for team leaders, R&D managers, and product managers who want to track the progress and state of the release through widgets; it includes Release Burn Down, Group Velocity, Release Backlog Cumulative Flow, and Feature Planned Story Points vs. Actual Story Points.

- *Scrum Master dashboard*: This is a widget collection for Scrum masters when managing agile Scrum releases and is more sprint-focused; it includes widgets such as Sprint Burn Down, Sprint Cumulative Flow, Team Velocity, and Team Workload.

To switch the Dashboard view to any of the options, open the Select Favorite options in the grid toolbar, expand the Public folder, and choose one of the options.

To further control the display of widgets on the screen, you can use the icon resembling a table's columns layout on the grid toolbar, which allows you to split widgets into groups of several configurations, such as 2 Columns or 3 Columns, as shown in Figure 6-2.

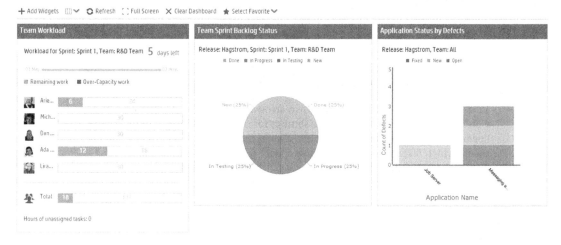

Figure 6-2. *Dashboard 3 Columns view*

Using the columns layout gives you great flexibility for the widgets because you can drag them across the different columns and rows. When you create your widgets, this will also prove useful because some widgets require more screen real estate than others.

Let's explore other grid toolbar actions that are available.

- *Add Widgets*: This allows you to add widgets to the current Dashboard view from the widgets collection and allows you to create and remove custom widgets.

- *Refresh*: Layout view doesn't automatically refresh, so to reload the widgets and refresh the view, click the Refresh button.

- *Full Screen*: Teams usually have a dedicated monitor on a wall to show the application and monitor system health, as well as show Scrum team updates. For this purpose and others, the full-screen button creates a minimal view of the page with only the widgets and the grid toolbar available.

- *Clear Dashboard*: This allows you to remove all widgets from the current Dashboard view and allows you to begin a clean widgets collection for a new dashboard.

Managing Widgets

Widgets are self-contained blocks of information, whether visual charts or another form of textual data, and they allow basic interaction with the plotted view. Once a widget is added to the layout view, it can be dragged to any of the columns, as well as moved up and down in the position ordering.

■ **Note** To drag a widget, hover over the widget's top title bar, which will turn blue; when cursor changes to the multidirectional icon, simply drag the widget around.

Widgets have basic controls located on the top-right side of the widget's title bar, as shown in Figure 6-3. Let's review the options.

- *Removing widgets*: The X icon will remove the widget from the view. It doesn't confirm this action with a pop-up of any sort, so be careful not to mistakenly remove widgets from your layout.

- *Minimizing and maximizing*: Clicking the - or + icon allows you to expand or collapse a widget block.

- *Displaying information*: Hovering over the *i* icon for each widget will show a tooltip with the description of the widget.

- *Widget configuration*: Clicking the down arrow will present a few options: Configure Settings to customize the settings for the widget, Refresh to reload the specific widget data, and Full Screen to extend the specific widget to Full Screen mode, which takes up the entire layout space. When in Full Screen mode, this option changes to Restore.

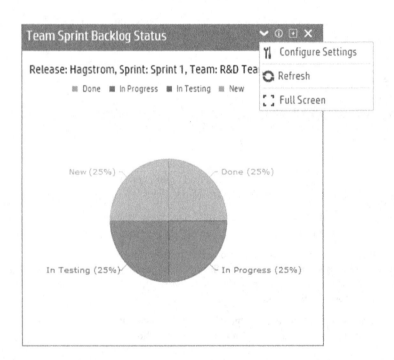

Figure 6-3. *Dashboard widget control*

Adding Widgets

To begin adding widgets to a layout, click the Add Widgets option in the grid toolbar. Figure 6-4 shows the pop-up window Add Dashboard Widget that appears. In it you can choose a widget from the built-in widgets library that Agile Manager provides.

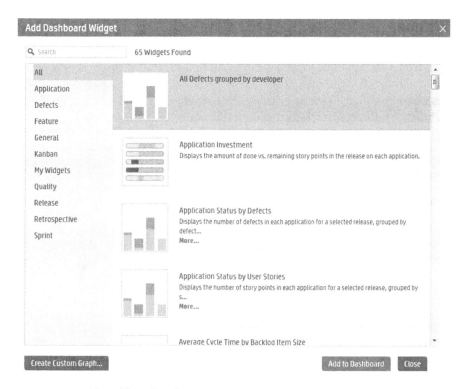

Figure 6-4. *Add Dashboard Widget window*

The newly opened Add Dashboard Widget pop-up window provides a Search input box to type keywords for quickly filtering through the listed results, and it shows the count for all found widgets. By default, the pop-up window will show up with nothing typed in the Search, but as of this writing, there are 65 available widgets to choose from.

The list of widgets includes a title, a description, and a picture to convey the type of widget displayed, such as vertical bar charts, pie charts, horizontal bar charts, or visual implementations.

Every widget belongs to one or more categories, as shown in the list of category tags on the left of the window. Clicking any category will filter the widgets search results accordingly.

■ **Note** Next you will learn how to create your own custom widgets; they too will be listed in the widgets search results and can be filtered and searched for.

Let's select a specific widget from the list to further customize the layout. From the widgets category on the left, choose Defects, and then choose the widget Application Status by Defects. To add it into the current Dashboard view, you should double-click the widget from the search results list or toggle the widget and then click the Add to Dashboard button at the bottom right of the pop-up window. The widget is then added automatically to the bottom of the Dashboard view.

Customizing Widgets

Figure 6-5 shows the widget you just added, displaying the distribution of defects and their severity per assigned developer.

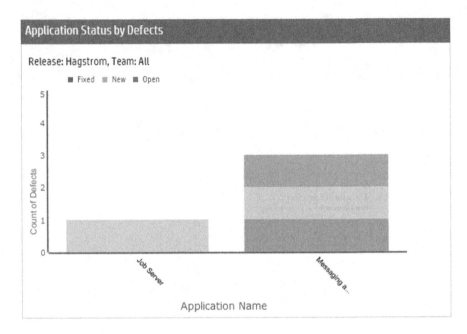

Figure 6-5. *Defects widget*

This kind of widget is useful for figuring out which application component may be suffering from low quality because of many defects. In which application does it take more time to close defects, or which application is easier to test and find defects?

What about if you wanted to take the concept of defects quality per application and apply it to developers? Then you could ask questions like, which developers are getting assigned the most defects? It may raise some important questions for managing your team and releases.

- Are the developers who are assigned the most defects the busiest?

- Are those developers delivering features with bad quality so they always get defects opened for their user stories?

- Are these developers busiest because their skill set and experience is the most widely required in the team's releases and features? If so, possibly you have a knowledge/ skill bottleneck and need to train other teammates to be able to take on some of this workload.

You'll further customize this widget to provide a real-time measure of currently open defects per developer and to show only those defects that are high or critical. This will give you a live view into the dashboard for the sprint or release quality with regard to currently open defects.

From the widget title bar, click the down arrow to show the actions available for the widget; choose the Configure Settings option. The widget's content area will change to the configuration wizard, as shown in Figure 6-6.

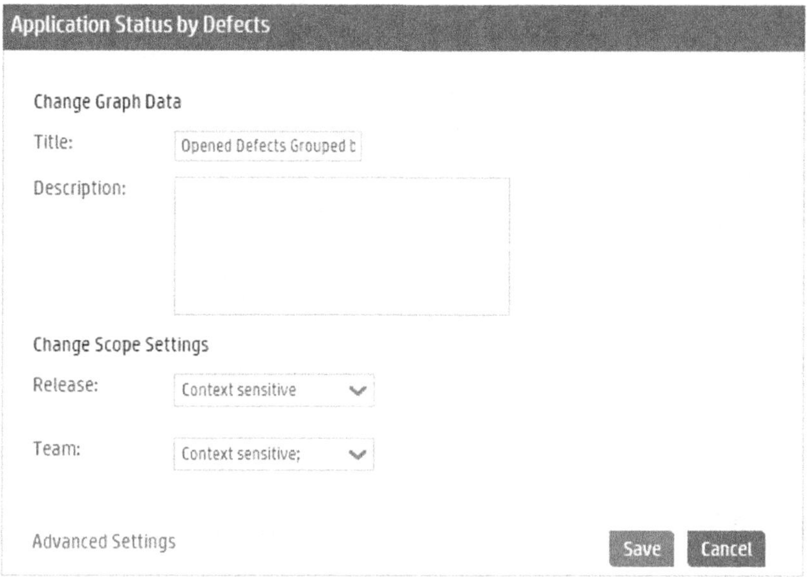

Figure 6-6. Widget configuration wizard

At this point, you can further customize the title and description as you please, which will save it as a new, custom widget. Set the title to Opened Defects Grouped by Developer and update the description accordingly. The scope settings are important, and the Release and Team scopes should both be set to "Context sensitive," which means that the widget will always display data relative to the release and team that you set in the top contextual filters for the Dashboard view.

Clicking Advanced Settings will open a pop-up window for more wizard-based widget configuration. Let's skip the Graph Type step because you already updated the title for this widget.

The Source Data step allows you to specify that defects from the backlog should be shown, so you can further skip to the Filter step by clicking the Next button on the bottom of the window.

Here, you'll remove the current filter Defect Status, as shown in Figure 6-7, and instead apply the following filter:

1. Click Add Property and choose Status. Once the filter is added, open the drop-box and toggle the New, In-Progress, and In-Testing options from the list.

2. Click Next, and you can proceed to update your view's display accordingly:

   - *X-Axis*: Assigned-To

   - *Y-Axis*: Count

   - *Group by*: Defect Severity

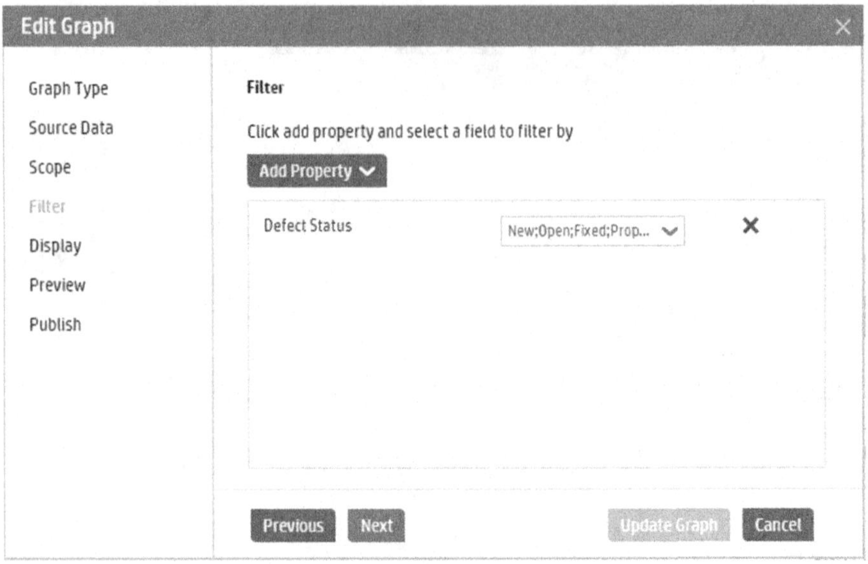

Edit Graph

Graph Type

Source Data

Scope

Filter

Display

Preview

Publish

Filter

Click add property and select a field to filter by

Add Property ∨

Defect Status   New;Open;Fixed;Prop... ∨   ✕

Previous   Next   Update Graph   Cancel

Figure 6-7. Widget configuration wizard, Filter step

The graph can remain as a bar chart, so you'll leave that chart icon toggled on and click Next to confirm; you'll see a visual representation of the updated graph in the Preview step.

To save and finish, click Update Graph at the bottom. Figure 6-8 shows the updated widget with your intended graph view.

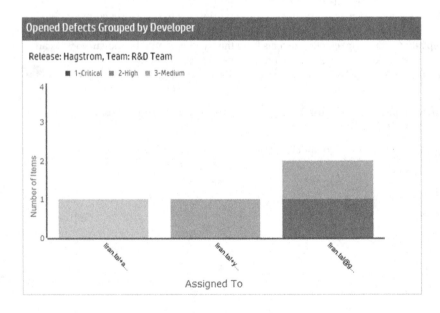

Figure 6-8. Customizing widget, finished

Managing Custom Widgets

Once you realize the flexibility of Agile Manager, you'll want to harness this powerful tool and the insights it can provide by creating your own custom widgets. Whether you're an engineering manager, QA manager, or developer, you'll find that working with a dashboard for agile workflows is a great way to assist you during sprints and releases, and it's even better if you can create your own custom widgets that show exactly the information you need.

Adding Custom Widgets

You'll create a custom dashboard widget that will show a user story's status per feature, and it will be context sensitive so that whenever you advance in sprints to feature freeze or to code freeze, the widget will represent the current state of features at that time. In closing, the widget will be able to tell you how many stories are currently in any state of New, In-Progress, In-Testing, and Done, per feature.

To begin, click the Add Widgets option on the Dashboard view toolbar and click the button Create Custom Graph, which is located on the bottom left of the pop-up window. At this point, the widget editing wizard will walk you through creating a custom widget.

Fill in the Graph Name field so it will create a custom widget with this name.

The Graph Type step, as shown in Figure 6-9, allows to pick either a summary graph or an agile graph. A summary graph shows the current state of backlog items, filtered, grouped, and presented using any of several charts, while an agile graph is shows a trend of backlog items. For your widget, a summary graph is the answer, so choose this option and continue by clicking the Next button at the bottom of the page.

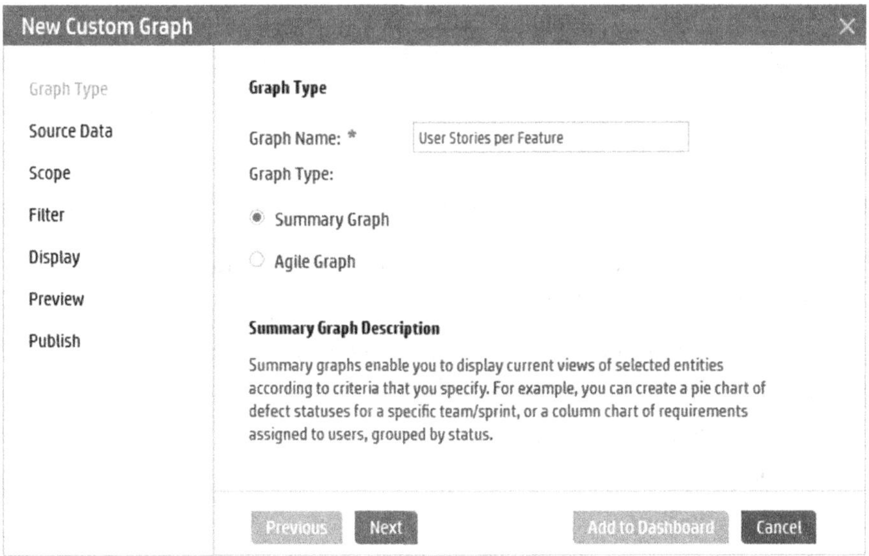

Figure 6-9. *Creating a custom widget, Graph Type*

The Source Data field is used to specify what kind of backlog items the graph is going to track. Because you defined that you want to track user stories, you'll use the "Select source data" drop-down options to locate the option called Backlog Items (User Stories); choose it and then click Next.

For the Scope configuration, since you're interested in presenting the information relevant to each sprint, you'll select the Sprint option. In the list, choose "Context sensitive release" and then "Context sensitive sprint." For the Team field, choose the "Context sensitive" option, as shown in Figure 6-10. This ensures that your widget will always reflect the dashboard's contextual filter settings.

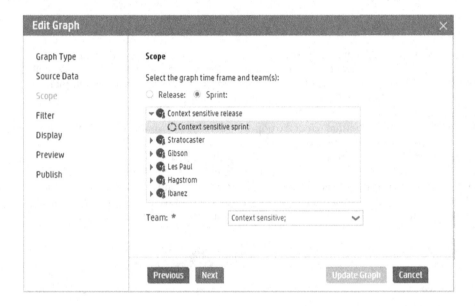

Figure 6-10. *Creating a custom widget, Scope information*

Clicking Next will take you to the Filter step, where you are able to apply any filters by choosing a field from the Add Property list to filter on. The sprint, release, team, and application are context sensitive, so there's no need to filter based on them, and although you don't need to filter based on anything in this example widget, you're welcome to choose any filter and set it up.

Continue to the Display step, as shown in Figure 6-11, which lists the available graph types. Several options exist; you can choose a bar chart, a horizontal bar chart, and a pie chart. Let's select the Horizontal Bar Chart icon, which is the middle one, and then set up the grid axis as follows:

- *X-Axis*: Set the Feature option.

- *Y-Axis*: Set the Count option.

- *Group by*: Set the Status option.

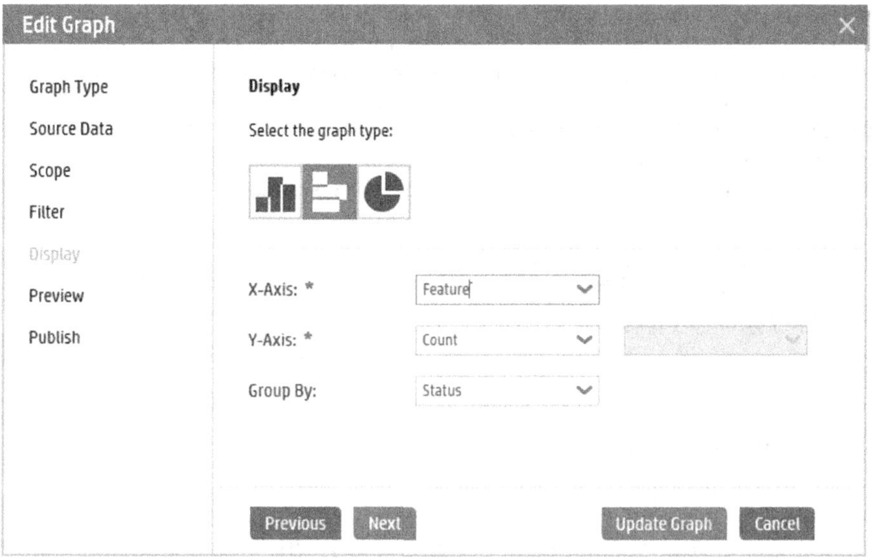

Figure 6-11. *Creating a custom widget, Display information*

Click the Next button, and you'll move on to the Preview step where you can see an example preview of the widget. The preview mode is useful because it allows you to play with the settings in the previous steps until you get it right and then continue with saving it.

You should be satisfied with the widget preview results because this is the user stories per feature widget that you were hoping to achieve. To continue with saving the widget, click the Next button once more.

The final step of creating the widget is all about saving the widget and publishing it, as shown in Figure 6-12.

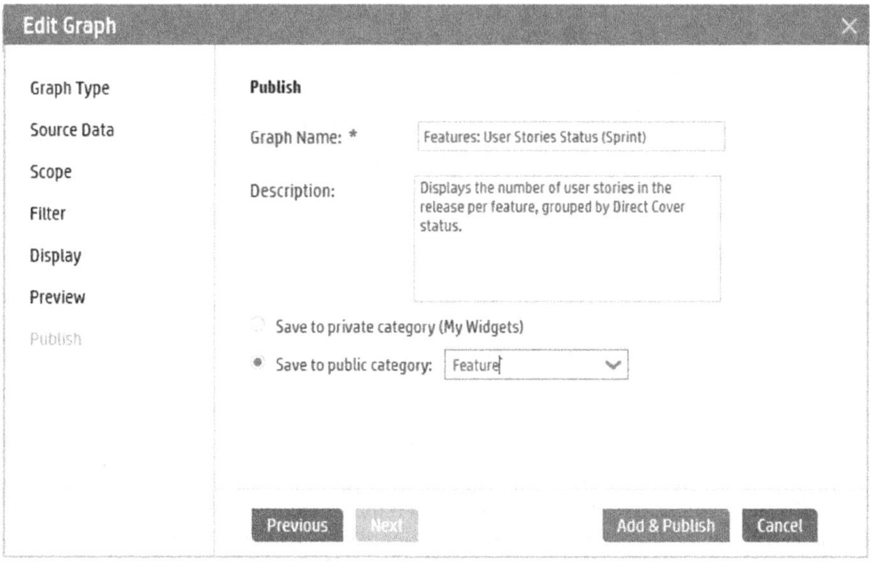

Figure 6-12. *Widget configuration wizard, Publish*

The Graph Name field is already populated with the name you set at the beginning of the wizard; you can provide some text in the Description field to describe the widget when it's in use on the dashboard. Finally, you can either choose to save the widget in a private category, so it is visible only to you, or you can save it publically so other users of Agile Manager can access it. When saving publically, it's required that you specify the category in which the widget will be available.

Once you've chosen whether to save it in a private or public category, click Add & Publish, and the widget will get added to the current Dashboard view and saved in the widgets library.

■ **Note** Regardless of the category you've chosen to publish the widget in, all of your custom widgets will always show up in the category called My Widgets.

Deleting Custom Widgets

You may want to clean up your custom widgets or fine-tune them over time. Beyond the configuration settings that are provided for each widget on the Dashboard page, it is possible to remove a widget completely.

To delete widgets, click the Add Widgets option in the grid toolbar, and in the widget library, first locate your custom widget. Then hover over it, and you should see an X icon to the top right of the selected widget. Click it to remove the widget and confirm the action, as shown in Figure 6-13.

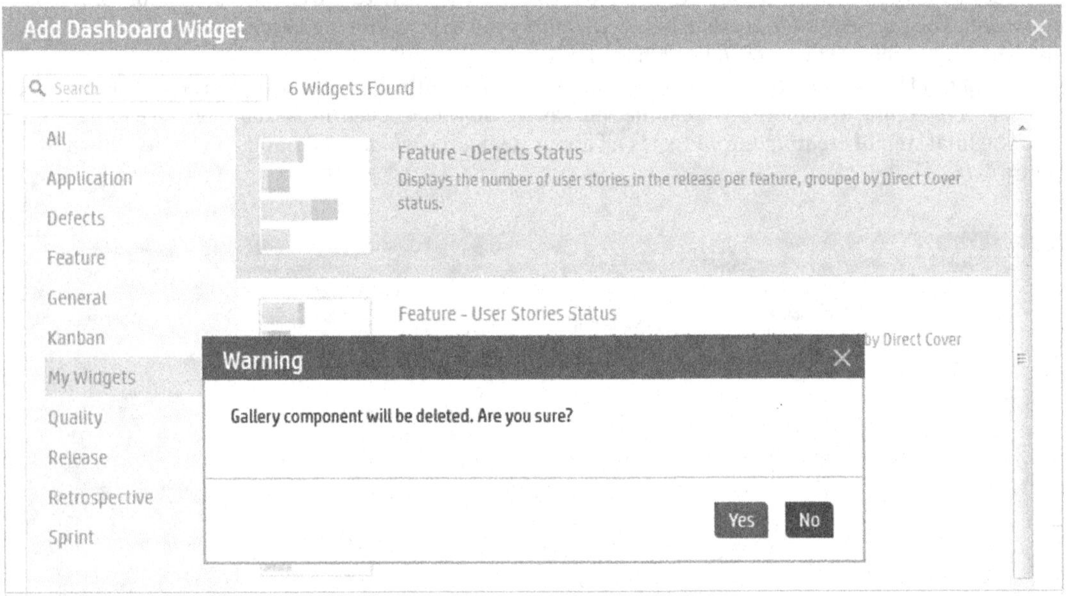

Figure 6-13. Deleting a widget

Once you have confirmed the removal of the widget by clicking Yes, the widget is deleted from the My Widgets library. If the widget existed in a dashboard, then it will remain available there, even though it was removed from the library. Removing the widget from the Dashboard view itself will completely remove the widget, without being able to access it again.

Reviewing Common Widgets

This section covers three useful widgets provided by Agile Manager that you might want to add to your dashboard.

Tracking Team Workload

It is quite often that as a leading manager or product owner you'd want to have a real-time view into the status of your R&D team throughout a sprint. Team members may also find it valuable to gauge their current status and be able to foresee any setbacks regarding time.

To add the Team Workload widget, click the Add Widgets option in the grid toolbar, and in the widget library, either locate the widget in the library, located in the Sprint category, or enter *Team Workload* to quickly search for it. Then hover over it and click Add to Dashboard.

As shown in Figure 6-14, the widget displays the current status through the following metrics:

- *Contextual information*: The widget specifies the context of the current status through the first headline. In this example, it is for Sprint 1 for the team called R&D Team.

- *Days Left*: This is the number of days left in this sprint. It will show 0 if the sprint is over and no more days are left.

- *Remaining Work and Over-Capacity work*: The availability of each team member is specified by a bar. A white, empty bar means the team member isn't allocated any work at all. Blue indicates the number of hours set in tasks across various user stories that are assigned to the user, and red indicates the number of hours set in tasks that are surpassing the number of work hours left in this sprint and hence are referred to as over-capacity for the team member.

- *Unassigned tasks*: If tasks are created for some user stories and the tasks aren't allocated to any team member, this will show the number of hours of unassigned tasks as the footer for the widget. This is useful information considering that it is often easy to forget to assign tasks to members, but AGM catches that for you.

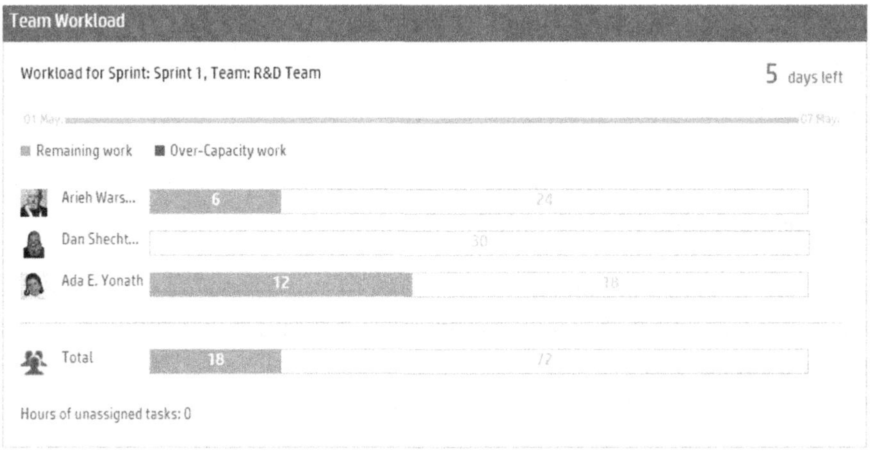

Figure 6-14. *Team Workload window*

My Defects and My User Stories

Other common widgets, My Watched Defects and My User Stories, are aimed more toward developers and quality engineers in the R&D team; they allow you to monitor and track the status of user stories and defects that are assigned to developers, or quality engineers. This ensures that they are always on track with their status and what is on their to-do list.

To begin adding these widgets, click the Add Widgets option in the grid toolbar, and in the widget library, either locate the widgets in the library, located in the General category, or type in *My Stories* to quickly search for it. Then hover over it and click Add to Dashboard. To track the status of your defects through other widgets, such as My Watched Defects, you can find it in the Defects category and add the widget to the dashboard as well.

As shown in Figure 6-15, the My Watched Defects widget displays a list of defects that you have set to watch; namely, it lists the following attributes for each defect:

- *Status*: Accompanied with an icon indicator, it displays the current status of the defect, whether it is New, In-Progress, or another state.

- *Assigned To*: This indicates the user to whom the defect is assigned, allowing you to essentially track and monitor defects that aren't necessarily assigned to you.

- *Modification time*: This allows to easily consult the last time the defect was updated.

- *Severity*: This displays the severity status field of the defect.

■ **Note**   The widget provides easy access to "unwatch" any of the defects in the list by clicking the icon to the right of each defect entry item. It also provides a quick link to view the defect item by clicking the defect ID to the left of the defect entry or to view all defects in the product backlog via the link in the footer of the defects list.

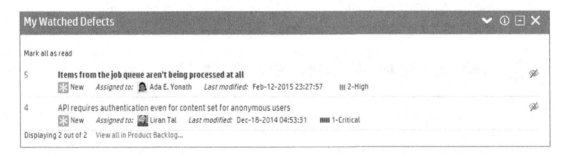

Figure 6-15. *My Watched Defects window*

■ **Note**   Another recommended widget that R&D team members should consider adding to their dashboards is Defects Detected by Me.

Release Backlog Cumulative Flow Diagram

A possible alternative to using a sprint burndown chart is a cumulative flow diagram, which can either aggregate the entire release backlog or show just the current sprint backlog. The diagram displays an area chart of the actual work items in different status states, with a y-axis displaying the number of user stories and an x-axis to show the timeline.

The cumulative flow diagram (CFD) is helpful to quickly view the overall status of a sprint or release in terms of whether the team is correctly handling the workload or whether more work is being piled on the team than it can actually handle.

To add the Release Backlog Cumulative Flow Diagram widget, click the Add Widgets option in the grid toolbar, and in the widget library, either locate the widget in the library, located in the Sprint or Release category, or enter *Cumulative Flow Diagram* to quickly search for it. Then hover over it and click Add to Dashboard.

As shown in Figure 6-16, the widget displays user stories in different states. The following are some key insights when reading this chart:

- *Items in Done*: These user stories will typically grow toward the end of the release, or sprint, as time progresses and more work is being completed.

- *Unmet Work*: The gap between the items that are set to New or In-Progress and the items set to Done is the work that hasn't made its deadline.

- *Work-In-Progress (WIP)*: The gap between items that are In-Progress (and In-Testing) and items that are Done is considered an approximation of the current work-in-progress load.

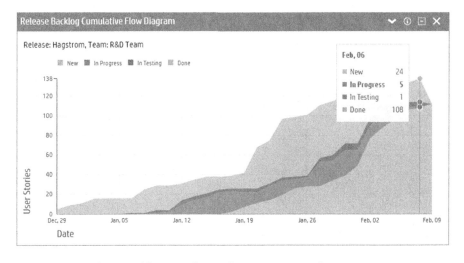

Figure 6-16. *Release Backlog Cumulative Flow Diagram window*

Summary

In this chapter, you learned how to build and set up an engineering manager's dashboard, which is also useful for project managers or any developer in the team to follow up on the sprint progress in real time. You learned how to add existing widgets from the library, as well as how to create and delete your own custom widgets.

CHAPTER 7

■ ■ ■

Helpful Resources and Support

In the previous chapters, you learned how to use Agile Manager. You learned how to sign up and create an online account, set up an application instance for managing agile software development for your team, and streamline the agile workflow for your team.

In this chapter, we will cover several resources for getting support when using Agile Manager, as well as familiarize you with educational resources that you can further pursue. Specifically, we'll cover the following:

- Support and the HP SaaS account

- Helpful resources for Agile Manager

Support and the HP SaaS Account

When signing up to use Agile Manager, you probably noticed that you signed up for an HP software as a service (SaaS) offering, called HP SaaS. HP SaaS provides more solutions besides Agile Manager, such as LoadRunner, which performs stress and performance tests on your infrastructure from the cloud, and many others.

The HP SaaS platform hosts your Agile Manager account, as shown in Figure 7-1, through which you can access any other products you sign up for. You're also entitled to get support from the respective product teams.

Figure 7-1. *HP SaaS account's product page*

If you need to contact HP's support for information or to report issues, navigate to Support on the main menu at the top and click New Ticket. You'll then be requested to choose which product to open a ticket for; click Agile Manager and choose a topic from the list or use the search to locate a topic, as shown in Figure 7-2.

Figure 7-2. *Issue search page*

To report an issue, click the Report a Problem link at the bottom of the left panel and choose the severity for it. Following that, the New Ticket page, as shown in Figure 7-3, will appear so you can submit the ticket.

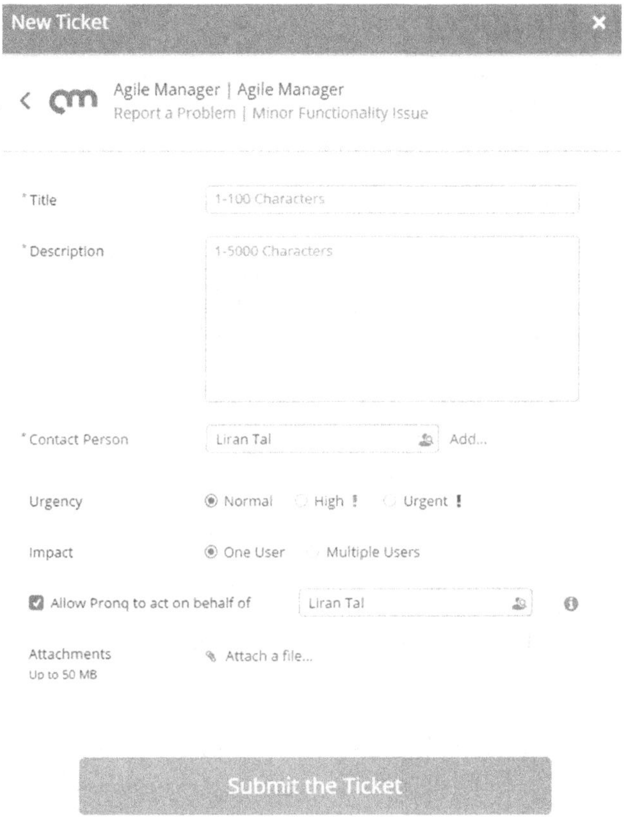

Figure 7-3. *Reporting an issue*

Once the ticket is submitted, you will get notifications via e-mail about its progress, and you can also track it through the Support area, as shown in Figure 7-4.

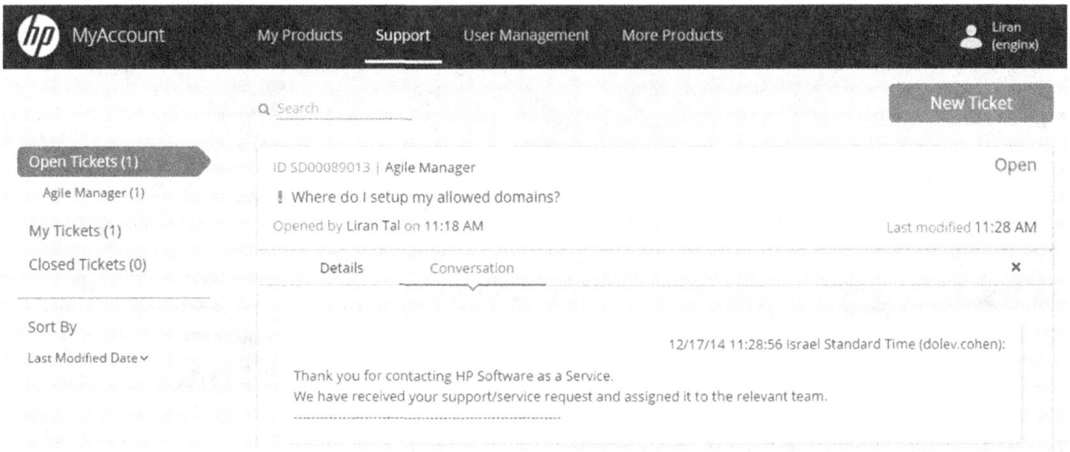

Figure 7-4. *Tracking open support issues*

Helpful Resources for Agile Manager

Agile Manager help is provided through several media channels, some of which are through an open community and forums board, and others are through official support and ticketing systems that are subject to licensing agreements by paying customers.

Agile Manager Community

The official Agile Manager community is facilitated on HP's Enterprise Business Community online digital presence (http://h30499.www3.hp.com/t5/HP-Agile-Manager/ct-p/hp-agile-manager), as shown in Figure 7-5. This online community support site features discussion forums for different aspects, such as the following:

- *Product Q&A*: Questions and answers (http://h30499.www3.hp.com/t5/HP-Agile-Manager-Product-Q-A/bd-p/hp-agile-manager-product-q-and-a)

- *Getting started*: Useful information and a discussion exchange for newcomers to Agile Manager (http://h30499.www3.hp.com/t5/HP-Agile-Manager-Get-Started/bd-p/hp-agile-manager-get-started)

- *Enhancement requests*: Where you are welcome to post any features you are interested in seeing implemented in upcoming versions of Agile Manager (http://h30499.www3.hp.com/t5/HP-Agile-Manager-Enhancement/bd-p/hp-agile-manager-enhancement-requests)

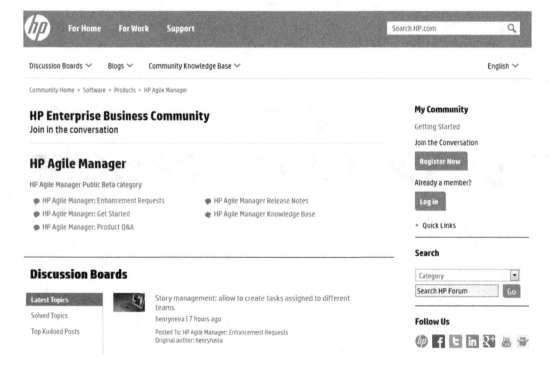

Figure 7-5. *Agile Manager online support community*

To take part in these discussion boards, you need to register to HP's Enterprise Business Community by gaining an HP Passport account, which allows you to sign in through the various HP web sites and online services. To create an account, click the Register Now button in the right column of the community home page, or navigate to `https://passport2.hp.com/hppcf/createuser.do` to create an account.

Agile Manager Video Resources

Because of HP's large presence and marketing effort in online media, a lot of content is available through social media, and YouTube in particular makes a good candidate for learning more about Agile Manager.

Most of the video resources on YouTube, as shown in Figure 7-6, are split between the following users:

- *HP SaaS*: This is HP's branded online presence. You can find a lot of Agile Manager video tutorials, overview, and news here (`www.youtube.com/user/pronq/`).

- *HP Enterprise Business*: This is HP's official channel for enterprise business. The number of videos is quite large, though there are also videos covering Agile Manager that are worth the watch (`www.youtube.com/user/HewlettPackardVideos`).

Figure 7-6. *Agile Manager video resources*

Agile Manager Help Center

Once you're logged on to Agile Manager's web interface, you will have access to its rich Help Center, as shown in Figure 7-7, which provides a manual and even links to videos about getting things done.

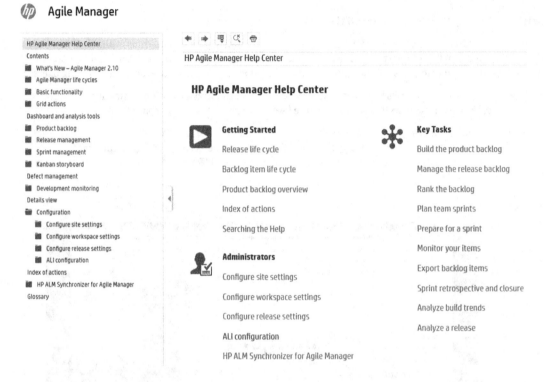

Figure 7-7. *Agile Manager Help Center*

To reach the Help Center area, hover over or click the question mark icon in Agile Manager, as shown in Figure 7-8, located in the top navigation bar at the right; then choose the Help Center option from the drop-down list.

Figure 7-8. *Navigating to the Help Center*

Summary

In this chapter, you learned how to get support for Agile Manager through official resources such as HP's SaaS platform and its ticketing system, as well Agile Manager's built-in Help Center. You also reviewed some publicly accessible and free resources on the Internet such as a dedicated YouTube channel with videos covering different features of Agile Manager, as well as community forums hosted and provided by HP for Agile Manager users.

Index

Get the eBook for only $10!

Now you can take the weightless companion with you anywhere, anytime. Your purchase of this book entitles you to 3 electronic versions for only $10.

This Apress title will prove so indispensible that you'll want to carry it with you everywhere, which is why we are offering the eBook in 3 formats for only $10 if you have already purchased the print book.

Convenient and fully searchable, the PDF version enables you to easily find and copy code—or perform examples by quickly toggling between instructions and   applications. The MOBI format is ideal for your Kindle, while the ePUB can be utilized on a variety of mobile devices.

Go to www.apress.com/promo/tendollars to purchase your companion eBook.

Printed in the United States
By Bookmasters